THE
POWER OF DUA

IqraSense.com

OTHER BOOKS BY IQRASENSE.COM

1. Dua for Success: 100+ Dua's (supplications) for success and happiness
2. Jesus – The Prophet Who Didn't Die
3. Summarized Stories of the Quran
4. Jerusalem is "Ours" – The Christian, Islamic, and Jewish struggle for the "Holy Lands"

THE POWER OF DUA (to Allah)

The Essentials of Making Effective Dua for Self and Others

IqraSense.com

Library of Congress Number: 2012908209

TABLE OF CONTENTS

This page is intentionally left blank.

1   Foreword

The intent of this book is to highlight the power of Dua – a power that many of us sometimes don't fully comprehend – because if we did, we would have done anything that is considered necessary to make dua work for us. Many of us make dua to Allah to ask for His favors, to get His attention, to seek forgiveness for our sins, or simply to get out of trouble, when we get into one. Sometimes, our dua to Allah brings immediate results; while at other times it doesn't. For those of us, who fully comprehend the dynamics of dua, the process can be straightforward and less stressful, but for others who don't understand it as such, the lack of results as we perceive them to be, sometimes can cast doubt on our faiths.

This book compiles divine guidance (Quranic verses, Ahadith, etc.) on the topic of dua and is meant to bring into limelight such topics that can make you understand the dynamics of dua. Again, when made properly, dua can transform our lives. However, as you embark on this understanding, you will find yourselves sometimes making certain changes to your life – a positive change – a change that can have far-reaching effects than simply getting your dua accepted for the short term.

You may have read a number of these Quranic verses and Ahadith of the prophet before, but here you are requested to constantly question yourself whether you indeed understand and apply each topic in your life or not. People's lives have changed when they have taken the time to apply the divine guidance compiled in this book.

You are encouraged to print the checklist page at the end of the book and post it in a place as a reminder to the topics in this book. That can help you focus on getting the gradual but permanent change that you need in your life.

This book doesn't claim to have included ALL the divine guidance on the topic of dua. However, an effort has been made to include as many references as possible. For any suggestions, you are encouraged to E-mail to admin@IqraSense.com.

May Allah help every one of us to APPLY what is in this book to our personal lives, to help transform words in action and to help inculcate a deeper understanding of this guidance in our lives.

IqraSense.com

2 Introduction

Dua – the act of asking Allah (God) – is about each one of us asking Allah (God) Himself directly for what we want changed in ours and in other people's lives. The goal of this book is simply to educate you and to provide you with enough knowledge to help make your duas effective. Probably it is more common than we think (according to religious guidance provided in this book) that our duas either remain suspended or are not answered - simply because we ignore a few basics.

If your duas are answered more than what they are today, it can have a miraculous or transformational effect on your life. In many cases, dua **CAN** change what is already decreed (see the explanation later in the book).

For those who make dua often but sometimes fail to see the results, the divine and religious guidance highlighted in this book will shed light on the reasons and what can specifically be done to increase the chances of dua being answered. The following pages delve into the various topics related to dua that can help you get a better feel for dua; how it is to be made; and what factors affect its acceptance.

3   The role of sins in bringing misery to our lives

Before we delve into the topic of dua we need to understand that trials, tribulations and challenges are part of every person's life. To counter that, Allah has provided us a very powerful tool – and that is the tool of dua or asking Allah for help and His mercy when we need it; and undoubtedly, we need it all the time.

However, to understand trials and tribulations that we face in our daily lives, we also need to understand the topic of "sins" and how the sins that we commit may be related to our trials and tribulations and also in the way of our dua being accepted.

The better we understand the ghastly nature of our sins, and the rate at which we accumulate them, along with their undesirable impact on our daily lives and the hereafter, the more it can propel us away from committing sins in general; and the more it will drive us to seek forgiveness for our sins – through making the right dua for us, as well as for others.

Ibn al-Qayyim, one of the very renowned Islamic scholars, provided one of the notable descriptions of sins and the impact of sins in this life and the hereafter. Here is a very short summary of what he compiled about how our sins impact our lives. [islam-qa.com]

- Sins deprive a person of provision (rizq) in this life. In Musnad Ahmad it is narrated that Thawbaan said: "**The Messenger of Allah (SAWS) said: 'A man is deprived of provision because of the sins that he commits.'**" (Narrated by Ibn Maajah, 4022, classed as hasan by al-Albaani in Saheeh Ibn Maajah).
- A sinful person experiences a sense of alienation (indifference) with his Lord, and between him and other people. One of the salaf had said that he could see the

impact of disobedience to Allah (in some aspects of his daily life).

- A person who commits sins finds things becoming difficult for him. In any matter that he turns to, he finds the way blocked or difficult. By the same token, for the one who fears Allah, things are made easy for him.
- 'Abd-Allah ibn 'Abbaas said: "*Good deeds make the face light, give light to the heart, and bring about ample provision, physical strength and love in people's hearts. Bad deeds make the face dark, give darkness to the heart, and bring about physical weakness, a lack of provision and hatred in people's hearts.*"
- Sins breed sins until they dominate a person completely and he cannot escape from it. Sin weakens a person's willpower. It gradually strengthens his will to keep committing sins and weakens his will to repent until there is no will in his heart to repent at all... so even if he seeks forgiveness and expresses repentance, it is merely words on the lips, like the repentance of the liars, whose hearts are still determined to commit sins and persist in it. **This is one of the most serious diseases that is likely to lead to doom. He becomes desensitized and no longer finds sins abhorrent, thus it becomes his habit, and he is not bothered even if people see him committing sins or talk about his sinful life.**

So, we can easily see that by engaging in sins, we are not only making the prospects of our afterlife (an integral part of Islamic faith) bleak but sins can greatly and actively contribute to the difficulties of our daily lives.

Allah says (interpretation of the meaning): "*Whatever of good reaches you, is from Allah, but whatever of evil befalls you, is from yourself...*" [al-Nisa' 4:79]

Whether we encounter challenges in earning a living, or in our family affairs, or in other matters of life, the burden of sins greatly inhibits us from seeking the ultimate blessings of Allah and to have the potential of leading a good life in this world and the hereafter.

As for making dua and the enormous potential it holds to help us ask for forgiveness and other things, the following pages provide a description of how we can maximize the use of this tool for ourselves and others and also to use dua to seek forgiveness- thus clearing our path for the good in this life and the hereafter.

4 Why making dua to Allah is not an option, but a necessity?

For those of us who only use dua when we are in dire need or difficulty, the reminders in this section prove that we should NEVER let go of making dua to Allah. This is because making dua lets us seek Allah's attention. Furthermore, dua similar to prayers is an act of worship that we simply can't ignore. Taking it further, by not making Dua, we make Allah angry. Consider the following sayings of Allah and the prophet:

4.1 Seeking Allah's attention

Allah says in the Quran (interpretation of the meaning): "Say (O Muhammad (SAW) to the disbelievers): My Lord pays attention to you only because of your invocation to Him..." [Surah Al-Furqaan, 25:77]

4.2 Dua is considered as an act of worship

The Prophet (SAW) said:
"Dua is worship."
[Narrated by Al-Tirmidhi, 3372; Abu Dawood, 1479; Ibn Maajah, 3828; classed as Saheeh by Al-Albaani in Saheeh Al-Tirmidhi, 2590]

Al-Tirmidhi narrated that Al-Nu'maan ibn Basheer (RA) said: I heard the Messenger of Allah (SAW) say on the minbar:

"Dua is worship." Then he recited the verse (interpretation of the meaning): "And your Lord said: Invoke Me [i.e. believe in My Oneness (Islamic

*Monotheism) and ask Me for anything] I will respond to
your (invocation)..."*
[Al-Tirmidhi said: a Saheeh hasan hadith]

4.3   Not making Dua makes Allah angry

The Prophet (SAW) said:
*"Whoever does not ask of Allah, He becomes angry with
him."*
*[Classed as hasan by Al-Albaani. Saheeh Sunan Al-
Tirmidhi, 2686]*

We, therefore, should not wait to build that relationship with Allah
that could be built through the channel of Dua. We should ask Allah
often, even if it's just forgiveness for our sins and thanking Him for
His bounties. Again, remember – ask Allah as often as you can.

5 What are Allah's and His Prophet's assertions about making dua?

Both Allah and His messenger (SAW) have repeatedly asserted the importance of making Dua. Consider the following sayings:

1. Allah's promise to the believers

Allah has asserted in no uncertain language about Him listening to our dua. Consider the following from Quran and Hadith:

Allah says (interpretation of the meaning):

> *"And your Lord said: Invoke Me (i.e. believe in My Oneness (Islamic Monotheism) and <u>ask Me for anything</u>) I will respond to your (invocation). Verily, those who scorn My worship [i.e. do not invoke Me, and do not believe in My Oneness, (Islamic Monotheism)] they will surely enter Hell in humiliation!"*
>
> [Surah Ghaafir, 40:60]

Allah also says in the Quran (interpretation of the meaning):

> *"And when My slaves ask you (O Muhammad (SAW)) concerning Me, then (answer them), I am indeed near (to them by My Knowledge). I respond to the invocations of the supplicant when he calls on Me (without any mediator or intercessor). So let them obey Me and believe in Me, so that they may be led aright"*
>
> [Surah Al-Baqarah, 2:186]

5.2 The Prophet's reassurance to the believers

The Prophet (SAW) also said:

> *"Your Lord, may He be blessed and exalted, is characterized by modesty and generosity, and He is so kind to His slave that, if His slave raises his hands to Him, He does not let him take them back empty."*
> [Narrated by Abu Dawood, 1488; classed as Saheeh by Al-Albaani in Saheeh Abi Dawood, 1320]

The Prophet (SAW) said:

> *"Allah is Most Generous, and He dislikes to turn away empty the hands of His slave when he raises them to Him."*
> [Narrated by Al-Tirmidhi, 3556; classed as Saheeh by Al-Albaani in Saheeh Al-Tirmidhi]

5.3 Dua is very dear to Allah

It was narrated that the Prophet (SAW) said:

> *"There is nothing dearer to Allah than dua."*
> [Classed as hasan by Al-Albaani in Saheeh Sunan Al-Tirmidhi, 2684]

This should leave no doubt in our minds about Allah listening to our dua and how He likes the act of dua. Let's not lose that opportunity.

6   How to Invoke Allah?

Allah has specific names that He has informed us about in the Quran. We, therefore, should call upon Him using those names. Consider the following:

1.   Calling by the names of Allah or Rahman

One of the well-known views amongst scholars is that Allah should be called using the names "Allah" or "Rahman".

Allah says in the Quran (interpretation of the meaning):

> **"Say (O Muhammad (SAW)): Invoke Allah or invoke the Rahman..."**
>
> [Surah Al-Isra', 17:110]

According to Ibn Taymiyah, the well-known view is that this is the dua of asking, and this is the reason for revelation. They said:

> **The Prophet (SAW) used to call upon his Lord, sometimes saying Ya Allah and sometimes saying Ya Rahman, so the mushrikeen thought that he was calling upon two gods, so Allah revealed this verse.**
> [Majmoo' Fataawa Ibn Taymiyah (15/10-14)]

6.2   Calling Him by His beautiful names

Muslims can also use any of the names of Allah when invoking Allah.

Allah says (interpretation of the meaning):

"And (All) the Most Beautiful Names belong to Allah, so call on Him by them, and leave the company of those who belie or deny (or utter impious speech against) His Names"

[Surah Al-A'raaf, 7:180]

7 What are the benefits and remedies of making dua?

Ibn Al-Qayyim (RH) said in Al-Jawaab Al-Kaafi [p.4]:

Dua is one of the most beneficial of remedies; it is the enemy of calamity; it wards it off, remedies it, prevents it befalling, alleviates it or reduces it if it befalls. It is the weapon of the believer. In the case of calamity, one of three scenarios must apply:

1. *It (dua) is stronger than the calamity, so it wards it off;*
2. *It is weaker than the calamity, so the calamity overpowers it and befalls the person, but it may reduce it even if it is weak;*
3. *They resist one another and each impedes the other.*

8   Why should we make dua, when everything is already decreed?

Many of us hold the view that why make dua to Allah, when He has already preordained all matters. Withholding dua with this idea (or any other) in mind is a serious mistake due to which we would be missing on the blessings of Allah.

It was narrated from Ibn 'Umar (RA) that the Prophet (SAW) said:

> *"Dua may be of benefit with regard to what has already happened or what has not yet happened, so adhere to dua, O slaves of Allah."*
> [Narrated by Al-Tirmidhi, 3548 and classed as hasan by Al-Albaani in Saheeh Al-Jaami', 3409]

In another hadith it says:

> *"The decree cannot be overturned except by dua."*

> [Fataawa Noor 'ala al-Darb by Shaykh Ibn 'Uthaymeen (may Allah have mercy on him)]

Shaykh Al-Islam Ibn Taymiyah said in Majmoo' Al-Fataawa [8/69]:

> *If a person says that he does not say dua or ask of Allah, because he relies on the divine decree, he is also erring, because Allah has made dua and asking means of attaining His forgiveness, mercy, guidance, support and provision. If good is decreed for a person he will attain by means of dua what he cannot attain without dua. What Allah has decreed and knows with regard to His slaves' circumstances and destinies is only decreed on the basis of means, and decrees will be fulfilled at the appointed times. There is everything that happens in*

this world or in the Hereafter happens on the basis of cause and effect; Allah is the Creator of both cause and effect.

Disregarding the principle of cause and effect is contrary to reason.

Shaykh Ibn 'Uthaymeen said in Al-Majmoo' Al-Thameen min Fataawa Fadeelat Al-Shaykh Muhammad ibn Saalih Al-'Uthaymeen [1/157]:

Dua is one of the means by which what is asked for is attained. In fact it wards off the divine decree and nothing wards off the divine decree except dua, and that may happen in two ways. For example, a sick person may pray to Allah for healing and be healed, and were it not for the dua he would have remained sick, but he was healed by means of the dua. But we say: Allah decreed that the sick person would be healed from this sickness by means of dua, and this is what was decreed. He thinks that were it not for the dua he would have remained sick, but in fact he did not ward off the divine decree, because the basic principle is that dua was decreed and that the healing would come by means of this dua, and this is the original decree that was decreed from eternity. The same applies to everything that is decreed to happen through some means or cause. Allah has made this means the cause for the thing to happen, and that was decreed from eternity, before it happened.

9 Can dua cause miracles to happen?

As mentioned earlier, dua can have a transforming effect and along the same lines can cause miracles to happen. As will be described later, Allah brought many miracles in the lives of the prophets, as described in the Quran. As Allah is the Supreme Being, He can make anything happen.

Al-Bukhari [933] and Muslim [897] narrated that Anas ibn Maalik said:

> *The people were stricken with drought at the time of the Prophet (SAW), so whilst the Prophet (SAW) was delivering the khutbah one Friday, a Bedouin stood up and said, "O Messenger of Allah, our wealth has been destroyed and our children are hungry, Pray to Allah for us." So he raised his hands [Al-Bukhari added in his muta'allaq report: and the people raised their hands with the Messenger of Allah making dua], and we did not see any cloud in the sky. But by the One in Whose hand is my soul, hardly had he lowered (his hands) but there appeared clouds like mountains, and hardly had he come down from his minbar but I saw rain running down his beard. It rained that day, and the day after, and the day after, until the following Friday. Then that Bedouin or someone else stood up and said, "O Messenger of Allah, our buildings have been destroyed and our wealth had been flooded. Pray to Allah for us." So he raised his hands and said, "O Allah, around us and not on us." Each time his hand pointed to part of the clouds they parted, and the clouds formed a ring around Madeenah. The wadis flowed with water for a month and no one came from any direction but he spoke of the heavy rain.*

In this context, let us review the story of what happened to the great Sahaabi Al-'Alaa Al-Hadrami, who was one of the most prominent scholars and devoted worshippers, one of the close friends (awliyaa') of Allah whose dua was answered. During the campaign against the apostates of Bahrain, he pitched camp, but before the people could settle down, the camels bolted, carrying away all the provisions of the army, including their tents and water, leaving them with nothing but the clothes they were wearing. It was night-time, and they could not restrain even one camel. The people were filled with indescribable distress and alarm, and some of them began making wills to one another (because they felt that death was inevitable). Al-'Alaa' called the people together and said:

> *"O people, are you not Muslims? Are you not striving for the sake of Allah? Are you not the ansaar (supporters) of Allah?" They said, "Of course." He said, "Then be of good cheer, for Allah will not forsake anyone who is in your situation." When the time for Fajr prayer came, he called the people to pray and led them in prayer, then he knelt up, and the people did likewise. He started to pray (make dua), raising his hands, and the people did likewise. They prayed until the sun rose, and the people began to look at the mirages caused by the sun, shimmering one after another, all the while fervently praying. Soon, Allah created a great stream of fresh water beside them. 'Alaa' walked towards it, and the people followed him, then they drank and washed themselves. Before the sun had reached its zenith, the camels started to come back from all directions, bringing the supplies loaded on them, so the people did not lose anything at all, and they were able to give water to the camels. This is one of the signs of Allah witnessed by the people during that campaign.*

[Al-Bidaayah wa'l-Nihaayah: Dhikr riddat ahl Al-Bahrayn wa 'awdatihim]

10 What if someone makes a dua about something sinful?

Do you sometimes make dua that involves a sin? If yes, then that's something to be avoided completely. How can one ask Allah for something that He, the Exalted, has forbidden us? Instead, we should ask Allah for showing us the guidance to stay away from such haram and sinful things. If we have to ask Allah through dua, let's not ask for what is forbidden, but let's ask to stay away from the forbidden.

According to Abu Saeed Al-Khudri (RA) said: The Messenger of Allah (SAW) said:

> *"There is no Muslim who calls upon Allah with a dua in which there is no sin or severing of family ties, but He will give him one of three things: either He will answer his prayer, or He will store up an equal amount of good (reward) for him, or He will ward off an equal amount of evil from him." They said, "O Messenger of Allah, then we shall say a lot of dua?" He said, "Allah is Most Generous."*
> [Narrated by Ahmad, 10709; Al-Mundhiri classed its isnaad as jayyid in Al-Targheeb wa'l-Tarheeb, 2/479; Al-Haafiz Ibn Hajar classed it as Saheeh in Al-Fath, 11/115]

Shaykh Al-Islam Ibn Taymiyah said:

> *The dua in which there is no transgression will be answered, or else the person will be given something equal to it. This is the best response. For the thing that he asked for may be unattainable or may be harmful to the person who prayed or to someone else, but he is ignorant and unaware of the harmful elements in it. But*

the Lord is Close and Ever-Responsive, and He is more compassionate towards His slaves than a mother towards her child. And He is the Most Generous, Most Merciful: if He is asked for a specific thing and He knows that giving it is not in the best interests of His slave, He will give him something of equal value, as a father does for his child when he asks him for something that is not good for him, so he gives him something of equal worth, and for Allah is the highest description.

[Majmoo' Al-Fataawa, 14/368]

11 Why a dua doesn't get answered?

Sometimes, dua is not answered. Some of those reasons eventually become obvious to us; while some do not. However, as Muslims we should understand such reasons, so as to help us better cope in situations when our dua is not being answered.

In this context, we should understand that just like each type of work and act of worship has certain etiquettes that need to be followed, similarly dua also has such etiquettes that must be adhered to for it to be answered.

We know from Quran and Hadith about the many reasons due to which dua is not accepted. Some of them are the following:

- The Dua that a person is asking may not be good for the person but that person may not know the reasons yet;
- A person's sins may be in the way of accepting Duas;
- A person earns his living through unlawful means (haraam means);
- A person may be asking for forbidden or sinful items.
- Etc.

In the Quran, Allah says:

> *"And it may be that you dislike a thing which is good for you"*
>
> [Surah Al-Baqarah, 2:216]

According to a hadith of the Prophet (SAW):

> *"There is no Muslim who calls upon his Lord with a dua in which there is no sin or severing of family ties, but Allah will give him one of three things: Either He will*

answer his prayer quickly, or He will store (the reward for) it in the Hereafter, or He will divert an equivalent evil away from him." They said: "We will say more dua." He said: "Allah's bounty is greater."
[Narrated by Ahmad, 10749; Al-Tirmidhi, 3573. Classed as Saheeh by Al-Albaani in Mishkaat Al-Masaabeeh, 2199]

On a related note, Umm Salamah said: I heard the Messenger of Allah (SAW) say:

"There is no calamity that befalls one of the Muslims and he responds by saying 'Innaa Lillaahi wa innaa ilahi raaji'oon, Allahumma ujurni fi museebati w'ukhluf li khayran minha (Truly, to Allah we belong and truly, to Him we shall return; O Allah, reward me in this calamity and compensate me with something better than it),' but Allah will compensate him with something better than it."
[Narrated by Muslim, 918]

Ibn Al-Qayyim said:

Whatever Allah has decreed for His believing slave is a blessing even if that is in the form of withholding; it is a favor even if that is in the form of a trial, and the calamity decreed by him is fair even if it us painful.
[Madaarij Al-Saalikeen, 4/215.]

Many ask if Allah is not being merciful with them when not answering their prayers.

What Allah chooses for His slave is better for him than what he chooses for himself. Allah is more merciful towards His slaves than they themselves or their mothers are. If something happens to them that they dislike, that is better for them than if it did not happen, so His decree is all kindness and mercy. If the slave submits to Allah and has certain faith that all dominion belongs to Allah and all things are under His command, and that He is more merciful to him than he is himself, then he will find peace of mind regardless of whether his need is met or not.

[Madaarij Al-Saalikeen, 2/215]

12 What are the etiquettes of making dua?

Just like there are etiquettes for most matters, dua has its own set of etiquettes that must be followed. The following pages shed light on some of those key etiquettes.

3.   Ask only from Allah

This may seem quite obvious but we should be sincere in relying on Allah for help rather than giving lip service to the issue. The more we rely on Allah faithfully, the higher the chances are that Allah will listen to our Dua. The Prophet (SAW) said:

> *"If you ask, then ask of Allah, and if you seek help, then seek the help of Allah."*
> [Narrated by Al-Tirmidhi, 2516; classed as Saheeh by Al-Albaani in Saheeh Al-Jaami']

Allah says (interpretation of the meaning):

> *"And when My slaves ask you (O Muhammad) concerning Me, then (answer them), I am indeed near (to them by My Knowledge). I respond to the invocations of the supplicant when he calls on Me (without any mediator or intercessor)"*
> [Surah Al-Baqarah, 2:186]

12.2 Precede dua by praising Allah and sending blessings upon the Prophet (SAW)

Another important etiquette for making Dua is that when making a dua, Muslims should praise Allah and send blessings upon the

Prophet (SAW). According to one of the hadith of Faddaalah ibn 'Ubayd, the Prophet (SAW) said:

> *"When any one of you prays, let him start by praising Allah, then let him send blessings upon the Prophet (SAW), then let him say dua however he wishes."*
> [Narrated by Al-Tirmidhi, 3477 and said: It is a Saheeh hadith. It was also classed as Saheeh by Al-Haakim and Al-Dhahabi agreed with him. From Zaad Al-Ma'aad, 1/257,258. Classed as Saheeh by Al-Albaani in Saheeh Al-Tirmidhi]

The Prophet (SAW) used to praise his Lord a great deal in his dua, to such an extent that it seemed that he could not praise Him enough. He said:

> **"I seek refuge in You from You; I cannot praise You enough."**

The Prophet (SAW) considered not praising Allah in Dua, as an act of haste.

According to a hadith by the Prophet (SAW) that was narrated that Fadaalah ibn 'Ubayd (RA), the Prophet (SAW) said:

> *"Whilst the Messenger of Allah (SAW) was sitting, a man came in and prayed and said, "O Allah, forgive me and have mercy on me." The Messenger of Allah (SAW) said, "You have been too hasty, O worshipper. When you have prayed and are sitting, praise Allah as He deserves to be praised, and send blessings upon me, then call upon Him."*
> [Narrated by Al-Tirmidhi, 3476]

According to another version [3477] of the hadith, the Prophet (SAW) said:

"When one of you prays, let him start with praise of Allah, then let him send blessings upon the Prophet (SAW), then let him ask whatever he likes after that." Then another man prayed after that, and he praised Allah and sent blessings upon the Prophet (SAW). The Prophet (SAW) said: "O worshipper, ask and you will be answered."
[Classed as Saheeh by Al-Albaani in Saheeh Al-Tirmidhi, 2765, 2767]

In fact, sending blessings on the prophet is such an essential part of Dua that according to a hadith, without this etiquette, the chances of Dua being accepted are very slim. Consider the hadith where the Prophet (SAW) said:

"Every dua is kept back until you send blessings upon the Prophet (SAW)."
[Narrated by Al-Tabaraani in Al-Awsat, 1/220; classed as Saheeh by Al-Albaani in Saheeh Al-Jaami', 4399]

According to another hadith from 'Umar ibn Al-Khattaab (RA), the Prophet (SAW) said:

"Dua is suspended between heaven and earth and none of it is taken up until you send blessings upon your Prophet (SAW)."
[Ibn Katheer said: Its isnaad is jayyid. It was classed as hasan by Al-Albaani in Saheeh Al-Tirmidhi, 486]

It was narrated that Faddaalah ibn 'Ubayd said: The Prophet (SAW) heard a man making dua after his prayer, but he did not send blessings upon the Prophet (SAW). The Prophet (SAW) said:

"This man is in a hurry." Then he called him and said to him or to someone else: "When any one of you has finished praying (and makes dua), let him start by praising Allah, then let him send blessings upon the

25

Prophet (SAW), then after that let him ask for whatever he wants."
[Al-Albani said: it is a Saheeh hadith. See Saheeh Sunan Al-Tirmidhi, 2765]

Shaykh Bakr Abu Zayd said in his book Tasheeh Al-Dua [p.23]:

The best category of sending blessings upon the Prophet (SAW) is at the beginning of the dua, in the middle and at the end. It is like wings for the dua with which it soars up to the clouds of the sky.

The second category is sending blessings upon him at the beginning and end of the dua.

The third category is sending blessings upon him at the beginning.

Abu Sulaymaan Al-Daaraani said:

Whoever wants to ask Allah for what he needs, let him start by sending blessings upon the Prophet (SAW), then ask for what he needs, then end his prayer with blessings upon the Prophet (SAW), for his sending blessings upon the Prophet (SAW) will be accepted, and Allah is too generous to refuse what comes in between.

This provides us with sufficient proof that we should always send blessings to our prophet (SAW) while making dua in order to get it accepted.

12.3 Ask Allah with humility

When asking Allah, we should express ultimate humility and humbleness, if we expect a response from Him.

Allah says (interpretation of the meaning) in the Quran:

> *"Invoke your Lord with humility and in secret"*
> [Surah Al-Aa'raf, 7:55]

> *"Verily, they used to hasten on to do good deeds, and they used to call on Us with hope and fear, and used to humble themselves before Us"*
> [Surah Al-Anbiya', 21:60]

Ibn Al-Qayyim said,

> *"...not being humble when making dua is a kind of overstepping the mark in dua."*
> [From Badaa'i' Al-Fawaa'id, 3/12]

12.4 Be focused and ask Allah with full conviction

When making dua, we should focus on the Almighty and His greatness and on His control over all the matters of this universe including answering our prayers. If we are distracted from Allah, the chances of our dua being accepted are very little as is obvious from the hadith below:

The Prophet (SAW) said:

> *"Know that Allah does not answer a dua from a distracted heart."*
> [Narrated by Al-Tirmidhi, 3479; classed as hasan by Al-Albaani in Saheeh Al-Jaami', 245]

For those of us who lose hope in the dua that we make or when we don't ask with full conviction is another reason that our dua to Allah don't get answered. However, when we make dua with full conviction, the chances of our dua being accepted are increased.

The Prophet (SAW) said:

> *"Call upon Allah when you are certain of a response, and remember that Allah will not answer a dua that comes from a negligent and heedless heart."*
> [Narrated by Al-Tirmidhi, 3479; classed as hasan by Shaykh Al-Albaani in Saheeh Al-Tirmidhi, 2766]

According to another hadith of Abu Hurayrah:

> *"Make dua to Allah when you are certain of a response."*
> [Narrated by Al-Tirmidhi; classed as hasan by Al-Albaani in Saheeh Al-Jaami', 245]

The Prophet (SAW) also said:

> *Allah says:*
> *"Indeed I am as My servant presumes Me to be, and I am with him when he remembers Me. So if he remembers Me to himself I remember him to Myself, and if he remembers Me amongst a company, I remember him amongst a company greater than it. And if he draws near to Me a span of a hand, I draw near to him the span of an arm, and if he draws near to me the span of an arm, I draw near to him the span of two outstretched arms, and if he takes a step towards Me I hastily step towards him."*
> [Narrated by Al-Bukhari 5/175; Muslim, 4/2061]

The Prophet (SAW) said:

> *"Allah, may He be exalted, says: 'I am as My slave thinks I am.'"*
> [Narrated by Al-Bukhari, 7405; Muslim, 4675]

The Prophet (SAW) instructed us to be more firm in our dua – meaning the confidence that we have in the acceptance of our dua. The Prophet (SAW) said:

"No one of you should say, 'O Allah, forgive me if You wish, O Allah, have mercy on me if You wish'; he should be firm in his asking, for Allah cannot be compelled."
[Narrated by Al-Bukhari, 6339; Muslim, 2679]

12.5 Have patience when making dua

As Muslims, we should be careful in not losing hope in our dua. We should also ensure that we don't get impatient by setting expectations for getting immediate results. The Prophet (SAW) said:

"You will be answered so long as you are not in a hurry and say, 'I made dua but I did not receive a response.'"
[Narrated by Al-Bukhari, 6340; Muslim, 2735]

Instead of being impatient, one should think positively and have faith and hope that Allah will make a way out for him or her. Being impatient will do nothing but increase stress and anxiety.

Allah says (interpretation of the meaning):

"So verily, with the hardship, there is relief, verily, with the hardship, there is relief."
[Surah Al-Sharh, 94:5-6]

The Prophet (SAW) advised Ibn 'Abbas (may Allah be pleased with him and his father):

"Know that victory (or achievement) comes through patience, and that ease comes through hardship..."
[islam-qa.com]

12.6 Be persistent in your dua

Being persistent means to repeat your dua to Allah and not give up faith or hope. This is proven by the Prophet's (SAW) traditions. Muslim [1794] narrated that Ibn Mas'ood (RA) said:

> *When the Prophet (SAW) made dua he would repeat it three times, and when he asked he would ask three times.*

Ibn Al-Qayyim (RH) said in Al-Daa' wa'l-Dawa' [p.25]:

> *One of the most beneficial of remedies is persisting in dua.*

In Kitaab Al-Zuhd by Imam Ahmad [305] it is narrated from Qataadah:

> *Mawraq said:*
> *I can find no other likeness for the believer except that of a man who is at sea, clinging onto a piece of wood, and saying, "O Lord, O Lord," that Allah might save him.*

12.7 Avoid haram food, provision and sins

One of the basic pre-requisites for having our dua accepted is to ensure that our way of life is devoid of haram (illegal) provision and food. This essentially means to ensure that the way we make our living doesn't involve haram. For example, if someone sells alcoholic products to make a living, that person's dua's according to Islamic teachings will not be entertained.

In a hadith it says:

> *The Prophet (SAW) mentioned the man who undertakes a lengthy journey and is disheveled and covered with dust, and he stretches his hands towards heaven saying, 'O Lord, O Lord,' when his food is haraam, his drink is haraam, his clothes are haraam. He is nourished with haraam, so how can he be granted a response?*
>
> [Narrated by Muslim, 1015]

Ibn Rajab Al-Hanbali (RH) said: It was narrated that 'Umar Ibn Al-Khattaab (RA) said:

> *"By avoiding that which Allah has forbidden, Allah will accept dua and tasbeeh."*

Ibn Al-Qayyim said:

> *Thus eating haraam things saps the strength of the dua and weakens it.*

How sins block our dua is something that many of us don't comprehend because if we did, we would pay more attention to stop the sins that we indulge in our daily lives.

Al-Qurtubi (RH) said:

> *It was said to Ibraaheem ibn Adham: Why is it that we supplicate and receive no response? He said because you know Allah but you do not obey Him, and you know the Messenger but you do not follow his Sunnah, and you know the Quran but you do not act in accordance with it, and you eat from the blessings of Allah but you do not give thanks for them, and you know Paradise but you do not seek it, and you know Hell but you do not flee from it, and you know the shaytaan but you do not fight him rather you agree with him, and you know death*

but you do not prepare for it, and you have buried the dead but you do not learn a lesson from that, and you ignore your own faults and are preoccupied with other people's faults.

[Tafseer Al-Qurtubi, 2/312]

13 What about the wait in getting the dua answered?

The "wait" involved in our dua being accepted sometimes increases our anxiety and stress. This "wait" is an opportunity for shaytan (the devil) to whisper doubts in our minds and hearts. The weaker our eeman (faith) in Allah and His religion is, the more we get entangled in this wait, thus increasing our anxiety and stress.

Ibn Al-Jawzi (RH) said the following about this subject in one of his books:

> *I think part of the test is when a believer supplicates and receives no response, and he repeats the dua for a long time and sees no sign of a response. He should realize that this is a test and needs patience.*
>
> *What a person experiences of waswaas when the response is delayed is a sickness which needs medicine, I have experienced this myself. A calamity befell me and I supplicated and did not see any response, and Iblees started to lay his traps. Sometimes he said: The generosity (of Allah) is abundant and He is not miserly, so why is there a delay?*
>
> *I said to him: Be gone, O cursed one, for I have no need of anyone to argue my case and I do not want you as a supporter!*
>
> *Then I told myself: Beware of going along with his whispers, for if there was no other reason for the delay except that Allah is testing you to see whether you will fight the enemy, that is sufficient wisdom.*

My soul (nafs) said: How could you explain the delay in the response of Allah to your prayers for relief from this calamity?

I said:
1 – It is proven with evidence that Allah, may He be glorified and exalted, is the Sovereign, and the Sovereign may withhold or give, so there is no point in objecting to Him.

2 – The wisdom behind that is proven in definitive evidence. I may think that something is good, but wisdom does not dictate it, but the reason for that may be hidden, just as a doctor may do things that appear outwardly to be harmful, intending some good purpose thereby. Perhaps this is something of that nature.

3 – There may be an interest to be served by delay, and haste may be harmful. The Prophet (SAW) said: "A person will be fine so long as he does not become impatient and says, 'I prayed but I did not receive any answer.'"

4 – The response may be withheld because of some fault in you. Perhaps there was something dubious in what you ate or your heart was heedless at the time when you said the dua, or your punishment is being increased by means of your need being withheld, because of some sin from which you have not repented sincerely.

So look for some of these reasons, so that you might achieve your aim.

5 – You should examine the intention behind this request, because attaining it may lead to more sin, or prevent you from doing some good, so withholding it is better.

It was narrated that one of the salaf used to ask Allah to help him to go out on campaign, but a voice called out to him: If you go out on campaign you will be taken prisoner, and if you are taken prisoner you will become a Christian!

6 – Perhaps losing what you have missed out on will cause you to turn to Allah and getting it will distract you from Him. This is obvious, based on the fact that were it not for this calamity you would not have turned to Him, because the real calamity is what distracts you from Him, but what makes you stand before Him is good for you and is in your best interests.

If you ponder these things you will focus on what is more beneficial for you, such as correcting a mistake or seeking forgiveness or standing before Allah and beseeching Him, and forget about what you have missed out on.

[Sayd Al-Khaatir, 59-60]

14 What is the best position for making dua?

Although, there is nothing stringent about the specific positions that we must take to make dua, there are certain positions that the prophet advised us which are better for making dua. The following ahadith advise us of those positions.

14.1 Being in a state of prostration

Making a dua in a state of prostration is highly recommended and therefore to make dua in a state of salat (prayers) is also recommended.

The Prophet (SAW) said:

> *"The closest that any one of you may be to his Lord is when he is prostrating, so say a lot of dua at that time."*
> [Narrated by Muslim, 482, from the hadith of Abu Hurayrah]

And he said:

> *"As for bowing, glorify the Lord therein, and as for prostrating, strive hard in dua therein because it is more likely that you will receive a response."*
> [Narrated by Muslim in his Saheeh]

14.2 Facing toward the qiblah (Kaaba)

Facing the qibla while making dua is another position that one should strive to take when making dua. Umar ibn Al-Khattaab (RA) said:

> *On the day of Badr, the Messenger of Allah (SAW) looked at the mushrikeen, who were one thousand*

strong, and his companions numbered three hundred and nineteen. Then the Prophet of Allah (SAW) turned to face the qiblah, then he stretched forth his hands and started to cry out to his Lord: "O Allah, grant me what You have promised me, O Allah, give me what You have promised me. O Allah, if this small band of Muslims perishes, You will not be worshipped on earth." He kept on crying out to his Lord, stretching forth his hands, facing towards the qiblah, until his cloak fell from his shoulders...

[Narrated by Muslim, 1763]

Al-Nawawi (RH) said in Sharh Muslim:

This shows that it is mustahabb to face towards the qiblah when making dua, and to raise the hands.

In Kashshaaf Al-Qinaa' [1/367], a Hanbali book it says,

The one who is saying dua should face towards the qiblah because the best of gatherings is that which faces towards the qiblah.

15 Can dua be said during salat (prayer)?

Although there is some disagreement on this topic among scholars, many say that there is nothing wrong in making dua within the state of salat (prayers).

Shaykh 'Abd al-'Azeez ibn Baaz (may Allah have mercy on him) said:

> *There is nothing wrong with saying dua during prayer, whether that is for oneself or for one's parents or anyone else. Rather that is prescribed, because the Prophet (SAW) said:*
> *"The closest that a person is to his Lord is when he is prostrating, so say a lot of dua then." ...*

He continued and said:

> *So if he says dua when he is prostrating or at the end of the prayer, for himself or for his parents or for the Muslims, there is nothing wrong with that, because of the general meaning of these ahadith and others.*
> [Fataawa Al-Shaykh Ibn Baaz, 11/173,174]

According to a hadith, the Prophet (SAW) taught the Sahaabah the Tashahhud, then he said at the end of it:

> *"Then let him choose whatever supplications he wishes."*
> [Narrated by Al-Bukhari, 5876 and Muslim, 402]

Ibn Abi Shaybah narrated in Al-Musannaf [1/331] that Al-Hasan and Al-Sha'bi said:

"Ask during your prayer for whatever you want."

It says in Al-Mudawwanah [1/192]:

> **Maalik said: There is nothing wrong with a man praying for all his needs in the prescribed prayers, for his needs in this world and in the Hereafter, when standing, sitting and prostrating. He said: Maalik told me that 'Urwah ibn Al-Zubayr said: I heard from him that he said: I ask Allah for all my needs when praying, even for salt.**

It was also narrated from him, i.e. Imam Ahmad that it is permissible to say dua asking for one's worldly needs and pleasures.

Al-Nawawi (RH) said in Al-Majmoo' [3/454]:

> **Our view is that it is permissible to say dua in prayer for that which it is permissible to ask for outside of prayer, of religious and worldly matters. So one may say: O Allah, bless me with good (halal) earnings, and a child, and a house, and a beautiful wife, describing her, or: O Allah, set so and so free from prison, and destroy so and so, and the like, and his prayer is not invalidated by any of that in our view.**

In Al-Saheehayn, in the hadith of Ibn Mas'ood (RA), it is narrated that the Prophet (SAW) said at the end of the tashahhud:

> **"Then let him choose whatever supplications he likes or wishes".**

And he (SAW) said,

> **"As for prostration, say a great deal of dua in it, because it is more likely that you will receive a response."**

Saying dua whilst prostrating is the best of dua, because the Prophet (SAW) said:

"The closest that any one of you may be to his Lord is when he is prostrating, so say a lot of dua at that time."

[Narrated by Muslim, 482]

16 What are the best times for dua being accepted?

The prophet (SAW) advised us of special times and circumstances for our dua being accepted. The following provide an overview of some of those special times and circumstances.

16.1 Making dua in the depths of the night

Dua made in the depths of the night has a great chance of being accepted. This is the time that Quran refers to as the last one-third part of the night, before dawn. At this time, Allah descends to the lower heaven to listen to the needs of the people praying to Him and to relieve their distress.

Allah says (narrated through the hadith):

> *"Who will call upon Me, that I may answer him? Who will ask of Me, that I may give him? Who will seek My forgiveness, that I may forgive him?"*
>
> [Narrated by Al-Bukhari, 1145]

The Prophet (SAW) said:

> *"During the night there is a time when the Muslim does not ask for the good of this world and the Hereafter but it will be given to him, and that happens every night."*
>
> [Narrated by Muslim, 757]

16.2 Dua made after the prescribed prayers

According to the hadith of Abu Umaamah, it was said:

"O Messenger of Allah, which dua is heard?" He said: "In the last third of the night, and following the prescribed prayers."
[Narrated by Al-Tirmidhi, 3499; classed as hasan by Al-Albaani in Saheeh Al-Tirmidhi]

This, therefore, proves that dua made at night, as well as after the prescribed prayers, is definitely heard by Allah.

The Prophet (SAW) said:

"Whoever goes to bed at night and says Laa ilaaha ill-Allah wa Allahu akbar wa laa hawla wa laa quwwata illa Billaah (There is no god but Allah and Allah is Most Great and there is no power and no strength except with Allah), then he says: Allahumma ighfir li (O Allah, forgive me), or he makes dua, his prayer will be answered, and if he does wudoo' and prays, his prayer will be accepted."
[Narrated by Al-Bukhari, 1154]

16.3 Dua made between the Adhan (call for prayers) and the Iqamah

It is narrated in a Saheeh report that the Prophet (SAW) said:

"A dua offered between the adhaan and iqaamah is not rejected."
[Narrated by Abu Dawood, 521; Al-Tirmidhi, 212. See Also Saheeh Al-Jaami', 2408]

This should provide us with another reason to pray in congregation in the masjid (mosque) and to get there early enough to catch the special time between adhan and Iqaamah to make dua to Allah with full focus and concentration.

16.4 Dua made at the time of rain

It is said in the hadith of Sahl ibn Sa'd that is attributed to the Prophet (SAW):

> *"There are two which will not be rejected: dua at the time of the call (to prayer) and when it is raining."*
> [Narrated by Abu Dawood and classed as Saheeh by Al-Albaani in Saheeh Al-Jaami', 3078]

16.5 Dua made on Friday

Regarding the day of Friday, the Messenger of Allah said:

> *"During it there is a time when a Muslim slave does not stand and pray and ask Allah for something, but He will give it to him," and he gestured with his hand to indicate how short that time is.*
> [Narrated by Al-Bukhari, 935; Muslim, 852]

This should enable us to maximize the times on Fridays to remember Allah through Dhikr and Quran and to make dua frequently throughout the whole day.

16.6 When praying (sending blessings) on Prophet (SAW)

As me mentioned earlier, we should send a great deal of blessings upon the Prophet (peace and blessings of Allah be upon him).

> *In Sunan al-Tirmidhi (2381) it is narrated that Ubayy (may Allah be pleased with him) said: I said: O Messenger of Allah, I send a great deal of blessings*

43

upon you. How much of my du'aa' should I make for you? He said: "Whatever you wish." I said: One-quarter? He said: "Whatever you wish, but if you do more it will be better for you." I said: One half? He said: "Whatever you wish, but if you do more it will be better for you." I said: Two-thirds? He said: "Whatever you wish, but if you do more it will be better for you." I said: I will make all my du'aa' for you. He said: "Then your worries will be taken care of and your sins will be forgiven." [Classed as hasan by al-Albaani in Saheeh Sunan al-Tirmidhi.]

16.7 Making dua with the help of the prayer of Dhun-Noon (Prophet Yoonus)

It was narrated in a Saheeh hadith that the Prophet (SAW) said:

"The prayer of Dhun-Noon (Yoonus) which he said when he was in the belly of the whale: 'Laa ilaaha illa anta, subhaanaka, inni kuntu min al-zaalimeen [none has the right to be worshipped but You (O Allah)], Glorified (and Exalted) be You [above All that (evil) they associate with You]! Truly, I have been of the wrongdoers.' No Muslim recites this dua concerning any matter but Allah will answer him."
[Narrated by Al-Tirmidhi and classed as Saheeh in Saheeh Al-Jaami', 3383]

The Quran states:

"And (remember) Dhun-Noon (Jonah), when he went off in anger, and imagined that We shall not punish him (i.e. the calamities which had befallen him)! But he cried through the darkness (saying): Laa ilaaha illa Anta [none has the right to be worshipped but You (O Allah)], Glorified (and Exalted) be You [above All that (evil) they

associate with You]! Truly, I have been of the wrongdoers."

So We answered his call, and delivered him from the distress. And thus We do deliver the believers (who believe in the Oneness of Allah, abstain from evil and work righteousness)"

[Surah Al-Anbiya', 21:87-88]

About this verse, Al-Qurtubi said:

In this verse, Allah stipulates that whoever calls upon Him, He will answer him as He answered and saved Dhun-Noon (Yoonus). This is what is meant by the words "And thus We do deliver the believers".

[From Al-Jaami' li Ahkaam il-Quran, 11/334]

16.8 Prayer of the oppressed, traveler, fasting person and a father's prayer for his child are never rejected

The prophet (SAW) advised us of people whose dua have a strong chance of being accepted. Those hadith are mentioned below:

In the hadith it says:

"Fear the prayer of the one who has been wronged, for there is no barrier between it and Allah."

[Narrated by Al-Bukhari, 469; Muslim, 19]

And the Prophet (SAW) said:

"The prayer of the one who has been wronged will be answered, even if he is an evildoer, for his evildoing is only against himself."

[Narrated by Ahmad. See Saheeh Al-Jaami', 3382]

It was narrated in a Saheeh report that our Prophet (SAW) said:

"There are three prayers that are not rejected: the prayer of a father for his child, the prayer of the fasting person and the prayer of the traveler."
[Narrated by Al-Bayhaqi. See Saheeh Al-Jaami', 2032; Al-Saheehah, 1797]

According to a Saheeh hadith:

"There are three prayers that will be answered: the prayer of one who has been wronged, the prayer of a traveler, and the prayer of a father against his child."
[Narrated by Al-Tirmidhi, 1905. See Saheeh Al-Adab Al-Mufrad, 372]

As stated in the hadith narrated by Muslim [1631]:

"When the son of Adam dies, all his good deeds come to an end except three: ongoing charity, a righteous son who will pray for him, or beneficial knowledge."

This hadith indicates that a righteous child's dua for his parents have a special significance.

16.9 When drinking Zamzam water

It was narrated from Jaabir (RA) that the Prophet (SAW) said:

"Zamzam water is for that for which it is drunk."
[Narrated by Ahmad and Ibn Maajah, 3062. Classed as Saheeh by Al-Albaani in Saheeh Al-Jaami', 5502]

This means that when drinking Zamzam water, one may make a dua.

17 What were the other special occasions during which the Prophet (SAW) made dua?

17.1 The six different places while performing Hajj

Ibn Al-Qayyim said:

> *His Hajj included six places where he stopped to offer dua: The first was atop Al-Safa; the second was atop Al-Marwah; the third was in 'Arafah; the fourth was in Muzdalifah; the fifth was at the first Jamarah; and the sixth was at the second Jamarah.*
>
> [Zaad Al-Ma'aad, 2/287, 288]

In following the prophet's (SAW) traditions, a Muslim should do the same.

17.2 During Circumambulation of the Kaabah

It was narrated from 'Amr ibn Shu'ayb that his father said:

> *"I circumambulated the Ka'bah with 'Abd-Allah, and when we came to the back of the Ka'bah I said: Will you not seek refuge with Allah? He said: We seek refuge with Allah from the Fire. Then he proceeded to touch the Stone, and he stood between the Corner and the door, and placed his chest, face, forearms and hands like this, and spread them out. Then he said: This is what I saw the Messenger of Allah do."*
>
> [Narrated by Abu Dawood, 1899; Ibn Maajah, 2962. Its isnaad includes Al-Muthanna ibn Al-Sabaah, who was classed as da'eef (weak) by Imam Ahmad, Ibn Mu'een, Al-Tirmidhi, Al-Nasaa'i and others. Shaykh Al-Albaani classed it as Saheeh in Al-Silsilah Al-Saheehah, 2138]

And he narrated that Ibn 'Abbaas (RA) said:

"The Multazam is between the Corner and the Door."

Shaykh Al-Islam Ibn Taymiyah said:

If the pilgrim wants to go the Multazam – which is the area between the Black Stone and the Door – and place his chest, face, forearms and hands against it and make dua and ask Allah for what he needs, he may do so. He may do that before the farewell tawaaf, for it does not matter if this iltizaam (clinging) is done at the time of the farewell tawaaf or at another time. The Sahaabah used to do that when they entered Makkah. If he wishes he may say the dua that was narrated from Ibn 'Abbas: "O Allah, I am Your slave, son of Your male slave, son of Your female slave. You have caused me to ride that which You have subjugated to me of Your creation and You caused me to travel through Your land until You caused me to reach Your house by Your grace, and You have helped me to perform my rituals (of pilgrimage). If You were pleased with me then I hope that you will be more pleased, otherwise be pleased with me now before I depart from Your House, for now I am about to depart if You permit, without turning to anyone but You and seeking to visit any house other than Yours. O Allah, give me good health in my body and protect my religious commitment; let me find my family well and safe upon my return and help me to obey You so long as You keep me alive, and join me, and give me the good of this world and the Hereafter, for You are able to do all things."

If he stands by the door and prays there without clinging to the House, that is also good.

[Majmoo' Al-Fataawa, 26/142,143]

Shaykh Ibn 'Uthaymeen (RH) said:

This is a matter concerning which the scholars differed, although it was not narrated from the Prophet (SAW) (i.e. that was not narrated in a Saheeh hadith, as the ahadith that were narrated concerning this were deemed to be da'eef or weak). Rather it was narrated from some of the Sahaabah (RA). So is iltizaam (clinging) Sunnah? When should it be done – upon arrival or when about to leave, or at any time?

The reason for this difference of opinion among the scholars is that it is not narrated in the Sunnah of the Prophet (SAW), rather the Sahaabah (RA) used to do that when they arrived in Makkah.

The fuqaha' said: He (the pilgrim) should do that when about to leave, and should cling to the multazam, which is the area between the corner where the Black Stone is located and the Door...

Based on this, there is nothing wrong with iltizaam (clinging to the Ka'bah in this area) so long as that does not involve annoying others.

[Al-Sharh Al-Mumti', 7/402,403]

18 Which is the best among the dua and where is it said?

When making Hajj, the pilgrim should make a lot of dua on the day of Arafah. The Prophet (SAW) said:

> **"The best of dua is dua on the day of 'Arafaah, and the best thing that I and the Prophets (AS) before me said is Laa ilaaha ill-Allah wahdahu laa shareeka lah (There is no god but Allah, alone with no partner or associate)."**
> [Narrated by Al-Tirmidhi, 3585; classed as hasan by Al-Albaani in Saheeh Al-Tirmidhi and also in Saheeh Al-Jaami', 4274]

It was narrated that 'Aa'ishah (RA) said: The Messenger of Allah said:

> *"There is no day on which Allah ransoms more of His slaves from the Fire than the day of 'Arafah. He draws close then He boasts about them before the angels and says, 'What do these people want?'"*
> [Narrated by Muslim, 1348]

It was narrated from 'Abd-Allah ibn 'Amr ibn Al-'Aas (RA) that the Prophet (SAW) said:

> *"The best of dua is dua on the day of 'Arafah, and the best that I and the Prophets (AS) before me said is 'Laa ilaaha ill-Allah wahdahu la shareeka lah, lahu'l-mulk wa lahu'l-hamd wa huwa 'ala kulli shay'in qadeer (There is no god but Allah, alone with no partner or associate; His is the dominion, to Him be praise, and He has power over all things)."*
> [Narrated by Al-Tirmidhi, 3585 and classed as hasan by Al-Albaani in Saheeh Al-Targheeb, 1536]

19 1The biggest mistake that people commit after their dua is answered

Acceptance of dua is a great favor from the Almighty Allah. So, it's only logical for us to thank Him for his blessings and bounties. Unfortunately, it is common for many of us to forget the time, when we were desperately calling on Allah for His help, and get so carried away with enjoying the results, that we forget remembering Allah and thanking Him for His grace.

Allah says in the Quran:

> *"He it is Who enables you to travel through land and sea, till when you are in the ships, and they sail with them with a favorable wind, and they are glad therein, then comes a stormy wind and the waves come to them from all sides, and they think that they are encircled therein. Then they invoke Allah, making their faith pure for Him alone, (saying): "If You (Allah) deliver us from this, we shall truly, be of the grateful."*
>
> *23. But when He delivers them, behold! They rebel (disobey Allah) in the earth wrongfully. O mankind! Your rebellion (disobedience to Allah) is only against your ownselves, — a brief enjoyment of this worldly life, then (in the end) unto Us is your return, and We shall inform you of that which you used to do"*
>
> [Surah Yoonus, 10:22,23]

Shaykh Ibn Al-Sa'di (RH) said:

> *They understood that they were doomed, so they ended their dependence on created beings and they realized that no one could save them from this hardship except Allah alone, so they called upon Him, making their faith*

pure for Him alone and promising that they would adhere to that, and they said: "If You (Allah) deliver us from this, we shall truly, be of the grateful" but "when He delivers them, behold! They rebel (disobey Allah) in the earth wrongfully" i.e., they forget that hardship and that dua, and what they committed themselves to, and they associate others with Allah whom they acknowledge cannot save them from hardships or protect them from difficulty. Why are they not sincere towards Allah in worship in times of ease as they are at times of hardship?

But they will face the consequences of their rebellion, hence Allah says: "Your rebellion (disobedience to Allah) is only against your ownselves, — a brief enjoyment of this worldly life" i.e., everything that you hope when you rebel and turn away from Allah, is to make some worldly gains, which will soon come to an end, then you will leave them behind: "then (in the end) unto Us is your return" on the Day of Resurrection, "and We shall inform you of that which you used to do". This is the ultimate warning to them against persisting in what they are doing.

[Tafseer Al-Sa'di, 361]

20 What should never be asked when making a dua?

The divine guidance provided above clearly shows that one can ask whatever they want to in time of need or at other times. However, there are stipulations about what one can't ask in a dua. The following hadith shed light on this issue.

20.1 Wishing for death because of a calamity that has befallen one

It is not uncommon for people to ask for death or to get suicidal thoughts. That is clearly against the spirit of Islam. In one of the Hadith, it is narrated that Khabbaab (RA) said:

> **"Were it not that the Messenger of Allah forbade us to pray for death, I would have prayed for it."**
> [Narrated by Al-Bukhari 6350; Muslim, 2681]

In another hadith it says:

> *"No one of you should wish for death because of some harm that has befallen him. If he must wish for it, then let him say: 'O Allah, keep me Alive so long as living is good for me, and cause me to die when death is good for me.'"*
> [Narrated by Al-Bukhari, 6531; Muslim, 2680]

20.2 Praying against oneself, wealth and children

When the Messenger of Allah saw a Muslim man who was sick and had grown feeble like a chicken, the Messenger of Allah (SAW) said to him:

> *"Did you pray for anything or ask for it?" He said: Yes, I used to say: O Allah, whatever punishment You would give me in the Hereafter, bring it forward in this world. The Messenger of Allah (SAW) said: "Subhaan Allah! You cannot bear it. Why didn't you say, O Allah, give us good in this world and good in the Hereafter and save us from the torment of the Fire?" Then he prayed to Allah for him, and He healed him.*

[Narrated by Muslim, 2688]

In the hadith it says:

> *"Do not pray against yourselves, do not pray against your children, and do not pray against your wealth, lest that coincide with an hour when Allah is asked and He answers your prayers."*

[Narrated by Muslim, 3009]

21 Can one say dua in one's own words and own language?

Although Muslims should preferably memorize the many dua for the many occasions that the Quran and the prophet (SAW) taught us, there are times when people have to articulate their needs in their own language or simply don't know the dua from the Hadith and Quran. During those times, people can ask Allah in their own language and words.

Shaykh Al-Islam Ibn Taymiyah was asked about a man who made dua in ungrammatical language, and a man said to him that Allah would not accept a dua spoken in ungrammatical language. He replied:

> *Whoever voiced this opinion is a sinner who has gone against the Quran and Sunnah and the view of the salaf. For whoever calls upon Allah, devoting his worship sincerely and purely to Him, calling upon him with a dua that is permissible, Allah will listen to him and respond to his dua, whether it is in proper Arabic or in ungrammatical language. The opinion mentioned has no basis, rather the one who makes dua, if he is not used to speaking in grammatical Arabic, he should not force himself to do so. One of the salaf said, if a person forces himself to speak grammatical Arabic, he will not be focused in his heart. Similarly it is makrooh to force oneself to make the words of the dua rhyme; if that happens spontaneously, then it is fine, for the dua should come from the heart, and the tongue should simply follow the heart. Whoever focuses in his dua on making the words grammatically correct will have less focus in his heart. Therefore the one who is in urgent need should pray from the heart with whatever words Allah inspires him to say, without preparing it*

beforehand.   This is something which every believer finds in his heart. It is permissible to make dua in Arabic or in languages other than Arabic. Allah knows the desire of the one who is making dua, even if he cannot speak Arabic correctly, for He understands all languages and understands the needs of those who speak different languages.

[Al-Fatawa Al-Kubra, 2/424,425]

22 Istighfar (repentance) as a form of dua

Isitghfar is perhaps one of the best tools that can be used to ward off problems in one's life. Istighfar is kind of a dua where a believer asks Allah for forgiveness for his sins (see the earlier section of this book on the topic of sins). The prophet has advised us to repeatedly say istighfar during the day as he himself used to say istighfar a minimum of 70 to 100 times a day. If he as a prophet sought Allah's forgiveness so many times a day, we definitely need to do so much more than that.

There are many accounts in Quran and Hadith that prove that constantly asking for Allah's forgiveness increases one's wealth, and wards off calamity. Consider the following divine guidance in the form of Quran, hadith, and interpretation of divine guidance.

Allah says (interpretation of the meaning):

> *"I said (to them): 'Ask forgiveness from your Lord, verily, He is Oft-Forgiving;*
>
> *11. 'He will send rain to you in abundance,*
>
> *12. 'And give you increase in wealth and children, and bestow on you gardens and bestow on you rivers.'"*
>
> [Surah Nooh, 71:10-12]

Al-Qurtubi said:

> *The words "I said (to them): 'Ask forgiveness from your Lord'" mean: ask Him for forgiveness of your previous sins with sincerity of faith.*

"verily, He is Oft-Forgiving" means, He forgives everyone who turns to Him; this encourages us to repent.

"He will send rain to you in abundance" means, He will send a great deal of rain to you

.

"And give you increase in wealth and children, and bestow on you gardens and bestow on you rivers"

Al-Shu'bi said:

'Umar went out to pray for rain and he did no more than pray for forgiveness until he came back, then it rained. They said: "We did not see you ask for rain." He said: "I sought rain with the real key by means of which rain is sought." Then he recited (interpretation of the meaning): "Ask forgiveness from your Lord, verily, He is Oft-Forgiving; He will send rain to you in abundance."

A man complained to Al-Hasan about a drought, and he said to him: "Pray to Allah for forgiveness."

Another man complained to him of poverty and he said to him: "Pray to Allah to forgive you."

Another man said to him: "Pray to Allah to bless me with a child." He said: "Pray to Allah for forgiveness."

Another complained to him that his garden was dry. He said to him: "Pray to Allah for forgiveness."

We asked him about that and he said: "This is not my personal opinion, for Allah says in Surah Nooh (interpretation of the meaning): 'Ask forgiveness from your Lord, verily, He is Oft-Forgiving; He will send rain

to you in abundance. And give you increase in wealth and children, and bestow on you gardens and bestow on you rivers."

[Tafseer Al-Qurtubi, 18/301-302]

Anas bin Malik (RA) narrated Allah's Apostle (SAW) said:

"Allah is more pleased with the repentance of his slave than anyone of you is pleased with finding his camel which he had lost in the desert."

[Narrated by Saheeh Al-Bukhari Volume VIII, The Book of Invocation, 6309]

22.1 Sayyidul Istighfar (Best among the Istighfars)

It was narrated from Shaddaad ibn Aws (RA) that the Prophet (SAW) said:

"The best prayer for forgiveness is to say: Allahumma anta rabbiy laa ilaaha illa anta, khalaqtani wa ana 'abduka wa ana 'ala 'ahdika wa'dika ma astata'tu, a'oodhu bika min sharri ma sana'tu aboo'u laka bi ni'matika 'alayya wa aboo'u laka bi dhanbi, faghfir li fa innahu laa yaghfir ul-dhunooba illa anta [O Allah, You are my Lord and I am Your slave, You have created me and I am faithful to my covenant and my promise (to You) as much as I am able. I seek refuge with You from the evil of that which I have done. I acknowledge before You All the blessings You have bestowed upon me and I confess to You my sin. Forgive me for there is no one who forgives sin except You]."

He said: Whoever says this during the day believing in it with certainty and dies that day before evening comes, will be one of the people of Paradise, and whoever says it at night believing in it with certainty and dies before morning comes will be one of the people of Paradise.

[Narrated by Al-Bukhari, 5947]

22.2 Other noteworthy Istighfars (words of repentance)

It was narrated from Abu Moosa Al-Ash'ari that the Prophet (SAW) used to recite the following dua:

"Rabb ighfir li khati'ati wa jahli wa israafi fi amri kullihi wa ma anta a'lam bihi minni, Allahumma ighfir li khataayaaya wa 'amdi wa jahli wa hazli wa kulla dhaalika 'indi, Allahumma ighfir li ma qaddamtu wa ma akhkhartu wa ma asrartu wa ma a'lantu anta Al-Muqaddim wa anta Al-Mu'akhkhir wa anta 'ala kulli shay'in qadeer [O Allah, forgive me my mistakes, my ignorance and my transgressing the limits of righteousness in my deeds and whatever You know better than I. O Allah, forgive me the wrongs that I have committed deliberately or mistakenly or jokingly, for all of that is possible in me. O Allah, forgive my past and future sins, what I have done secretly and openly, for You are the One Who brings (some people) forward and puts (others) back, and You are able to do all things]."

[Narrated by Al-Bukhari, 6035; Muslim, 2719]

It was narrated that Ibn 'Umar said:

We used to count that the Messenger of Allah (SAW) said one hundred times in a gathering: "Rabb ighfir li wa tub 'alayya innaka anta Al-Tawwaab ul-Raheem (O Allah forgive me and accept my repentance, for You are the Accepter of repentance, the Most Merciful).

[Narrated by Al-Tirmidhi, 3434, where it says Al-Tawwaab Al-Ghafoor (the Accepter of repentance, the Oft-Forgiving); Abu Dawood, 1516; Ibn Maajah, 3814]

It was narrated from Abu Yasaar that the Prophet (SAW) said:

"Whoever says astaghfir Allah Al-'Azeem alladhi laa ilaaha illa huwa Al-Hayyu Al-Qayyoom wa atoobu ilayhi (I ask forgiveness of Allah the Almighty, besides Whom there is no god, the Ever-Living, the Eternal, and I repent to Him), will be forgiven even if his sin is fleeing from the battlefield (a major sin)."

[Narrated by Al-Tirmidhi, 3577; Abu Dawood, 1517]

It was narrated from Abu Bakr Al-Siddeeq (RA) that he said to the Messenger of Allah:

"Teach me a dua which I may recite in my prayer." He said: *"Say: Allahumma inni zalamtu nafsi zulman katheeran wa laa yaghfir ul-dhunooba illa anta faghfir li maghfiratan min 'indaka warhamni innaka anta Al-Ghafoor Al-Raheem (O Allah, I have wronged myself greatly and no one forgives sins but You, so grant me forgiveness from You and have mercy on me, for You are the Oft-Forgiving, Most Merciful)."*

[Narrated by Al-Bukhari, 799; Muslim, 2705]

23 Is dua allowed at other people's graves?

People are often confused about whether it is acceptable to make dua at the graves or not. The scholars' accounts clearly show that it depends on the intent of making dua at the graves. If the dua is made for the deceased, then that is acceptable. However, if someone visits the grave with the intent to use the deceased person for seeking intercession to Allah, then that is completely forbidden. Unfortunately, this practice is quite common in many Muslim countries where people visit the graves of people and scholars believing that asking dua through them or at their burial sites will increase the chances of their dua being accepted. That clearly is a mistaken belief according to the scholars of Sunnah.

Ibn Taymiyah (RH) said in Majmoo' Al-Fataawa [27/165]:

> *As for visiting graves in order to make dua beside them or to seek to draw closer to Allah through them (tawassul) or to seek intercession through them, this is not taught by Islam at all. Hence the Sunnah according to the Sahaabah and the imams of the Muslims when a person sends salaams upon the Prophet (SAW) and his two companions (i.e., Abu Bakr and 'Umar, whose graves are adjacent to that of the Prophet (SAW)) is to say dua to Allah facing the qiblah, and not to say dua facing the grave. I do not know of any imams who disputed the fact that the Sunnah is to face the qiblah at the time of saying dua, and not to face the grave of the Prophet (SAW).*

However, when saying dua for the deceased, it is acceptable. Shaykh 'Abd Al-'Azeez ibn Baaz (RH) said:

.... one may say dua for the deceased facing the qiblah or facing the grave, because the Prophet (SAW) stood over graves after the burial and said:

"Pray for forgiveness for your brother and ask that he be made steadfast, for even now he is being questioned."

[Narrated by Al-Bukhari]

24 What about wiping one's face after making dua?

It is quite common for many of us to wipe our faces with our hands once we are done with making dua. By reading some of the famous scholars' accounts, it seems that there is not enough support for such a practice. Consider the accounts of famous scholars as indicated below. Furthermore, you are encouraged to ask other learned scholars for such matters as they may have more evidence from the Sunnah and there may be varying interpretations on this issue.

Imam Ahmad ibn Hanbal said:

> *It is not known that anyone used to wipe his face after making dua except Al-Hasan.*
>
> [Al-'ILAL Al-Mutanaahiyah, 2/840,841]

Shaykh Al-Islam Ibn Taymiyah said:

> *With regard to the Prophet (SAW) raising his hands when saying dua, there are many Saheeh ahadith concerning this, but as for his wiping his face with his hands, there are only one or two hadiths concerning that, and they cannot be taken as evidence.*
>
> [Majmoo' Al-Fataawa, 22/519]

Al-'Izz ibn 'Abd Al-Salaam said:

> *No one wipes his face with his hands after saying dua except one who is ignorant.*
>
> [Fataawa Al-'Izz ibn 'Abd Al-Salaam, p. 47]

25 Being careful about ones spoken words

When asking Allah or in other circumstances when we say anything, let's be careful in what we say and how we say certain things. Sometimes in anger we may end up saying what we really don't mean to say. The following hadith narrated from Abu Hurayrah shows that Allah takes into account of all things that we say.

The Prophet (SAW) said:

> *"A person may speak a word that pleases Allah and not pay any attention to it, but Allah raises him many degrees in status thereby. And a person may speak a word that angers Allah and not pay any attention to it, and He may throw him into Hell because of it."*

> [Narrated by Al-Bukhari, 6113]

26 Dhikr as a form of dua and its impact on the dua

Dhikr-Allah (remembrance of Allah) is one of the best deeds by means of which one may draw closer to Him. Once we are closer to Allah and build that relationship with Him, Allah will listen to us more. There are numerous evidences and proofs from the Quran and Sunnah (ahadith) about the immeasurable benefits of Dhikr.

Allah says (interpretation of the meaning):

> *"... Verily, in the remembrance of Allah do hearts find rest."*
> [Surah Al-Ra'd, 13:28]

The remainder of this section highlights the various verses from Quran and prophet's sayings on the benefits of Dhikr and it's power to bring us closer to Allah.

26.1 Allah's statements on the importance of dhikr

> *"Invoke your Lord with humility and in secret. He likes not the aggressors."*
> [Surah Al-Araf, 7:55]

> *"And (all) the Most Beautiful Names belong to Allah, so call on Him by them, and leave the company of those who belie or deny (or utter impious speech against) His Names. They will be requited for what they used to do."*
> [Surah Al-Araf, 7:180]

> *"Those who believe (in the Oneness of Allah) and whose hearts are set at rest by the remembrance of Allah; now*

surely by Allah's remembrance are the hearts set at rest."

[Surah Ar-Rad, 13:28]

"Verily, We, it is We Who have sent down the 'Dhikr' (the Quran) and surely, We will guard it (from corruption)."

[Surah Al-Hijr, 15:9]

"So glorify the praises of your Lord, and be of those who prostrate themselves (to Him)."

[Surah Al-Hijr, 15:98]

"Say (O Muhammad): 'Invoke Allah or invoke the Most Gracious (Allah), by whatever name you invoke Him (it is the same), for to Him belong the Best Names. And offer your Salath (prayer) neither Aloud nor in a low voice, but follow a way between."

[Surah Al-Isra, 17:110]

"And keep yourself (O Muhammad) patiently with those who call on their Lord (i.e. your companions who remember their Lord with glorification, praising in prayers, and other righteous deeds) morning and afternoon, seeking His face; and let not your eyes overlook them, desiring the pomp and glitter of the life of the world; and obey not him whose heart We have made heedless of Our remembrance, and who follows his own lusts, and whose affair (deeds) has been lost."

[Surah Al-Kahf, 18:28]

"In houses (mosques) which Allah has ordered to be raised (to be cleaned, and to be honored), in them His Name is remembered [i.e. Adhan, Iqamah,SAlat (prayers), invocations, recitation of the Quran etc.]. Therein glorify Him (Allah) in the mornings and in the afternoons or the evenings.

[Surah An-Nur, 24:36]

"Men, whom neither trade nor sale (business) diverts from remembrance of Allah (with heart and tongue), nor from performing As-Salat (Iqamat-as-Salat), nor from giving the Zakat. They fear a Day when hearts and eyes will be over turned (out of the horror of the torment of the Day of Resurrection).
[Surah An-Nur, 24:37]

"And put your trust (O Muhammad) in the Ever Living One Who dies not, and glorify His Praises, and Sufficient is He as the All- Knower of the sins of His slaves."
[Surah Al-Furqan, 25:58]

"Except those who believe (in the Oneness of Allah), and do righteous deeds, and remember Allah much, and vindicate themselves after they have been wronged. And those who do wrong will come to know by what overturning they will be overturned."
[Surah Ash-Shu'ara, 26:227]

"Recite (O Muhammad) that which has been revealed to you of the Book and keep up prayer; surely prayer keeps (one) away from indecency and evil, and certainly the remembrance of Allah is the greatest, and Allah knows what you do."
[Surah Al-Ankabut, 29:45]

"Their sides forsake their beds, to invoke their Lord in fear and hope, and they spend (in charity in Allah's Cause) out of what We have bestowed on them."
[Surah As-Sajdah, 32:16]

"Indeed in the Messenger of Allah (Muhammad) you have a good example to follow for him who hopes for

(the Meeting with) Allah and the Last Day, and remembers Allah much."
[Surah Al-Ahzab, 33:21]

"............and the men and the women who remember Allah much with their hearts and tongues Allah has prepared for them forgiveness and a great reward."
[Surah Al-Ahzab, 33:35]

"O you, who believe! Remember Allah with much remembrance."
[Surah Al-Ahzab, 33:41]

"And glorify His Praises morning and evening."
[Surah Al-Ahzab, 33:42]

"Those (angels) who bear the Throne (of Allah) and those around it glorify the praises of their Lord, and believe in Him, and ask forgiveness for those who believe (in the Oneness of Allah) (saying): "Our Lord! You comprehend all things in mercy and knowledge, so forgive those who repent and follow Your way, and save them from the torment of the blazing Fire!"
[Surah Ghafir, 40:7]

"He is the Ever-Living; so invoke Him making your worship pure for Him alone. All the praises and thanks are to Allah, the Lord of the worlds."
[Surah Ghafir, 40:65]

"And who speaks better than he who calls to Allah while he himself does good, and says: 'I am surely of those who submit'?"
[Surah Fussilat, 41:33]

"But if they are too proud (to do so), then there are those who are with your Lord (angels) glorify Him night and day, and never are they tired."

[Surah Fussilat, 41:38]

"And whoever turns himself away from the remembrance of the Most Gracious Allah, We appoint for him a Shaitan, so he becomes his associate."

[Surah Az-Zukhruf, 43:36]

"And glorify Him in the night and after the prayers."

[Surah Qaf, 50:40]

"And wait patiently for the judgement of your Lord, for surely you are before Our eyes, and sing the praise of your Lord when you rise;"

[Surah At-Tur, 52:48]

"And in the night, give Him glory too, and at the setting of the stars."

[Surah At-Tur, 52:49]

"Then glorify with praises the Name of your Lord, the Most Great."

[Surah Al-Waqi'ah, 56:74]

"So glorify with praises the Name of your Lord, the Most Great."

[Surah Al-Waqi'ah, 56:96]

"Whatsoever is in the heavens and the earth glorifies Allah - and He is the All-Mighty, All-Wise."

[Surah Al-Hadid, 57:1]

"Has not the time yet come for those who believe that their hearts should be humble for the remembrance of Allah and what has come down of the truth? And (that)

they should not be like those who were given the Book before, but the time became prolonged to them, so their hearts hardened, and most of them are transgressors."

[Surah Al-Hadid, 57:16]

"He is Allah, the Creator, the Maker, the Bestower of forms; His are the most excellent names; whatever is in the heavens and the earth declares His glory; and He is the All-Mighty, All-Wise."

[Surah Al-Hashr, 59:24]

"Whatever is in the heavens and whatever is in the earth declares the glory of Allah; and He is the All-Mighty, All-Wise."

[Surah As-Saff, 61:1]

"Whatever is in the heavens and whatever is in the earth declares the glory of Allah, the King, the Holy, the All-Mighty, the All-Wise."

[Surah Al-Jumu'ah, 62:1]

"Then when the (Jumuah) Salath is ended, you may disperse through the land, and seek the Bounty of Allah, (by working etc.) and remember Allah much; that you may be successful."

[Surah Al-Jumu'ah, 62:10]

"Therefore glorify the Name of your Lord, the Most Great."

[Surah Al-Haqqah, 69:52]

"And glorify the Name of your Lord, morning and evening."

[Surah Al-Insan, 76:25]

"He indeed shall be successful who purifies himself, and magnifies the name of his Lord and prays."

[Surah Al-A'la, 87:14,15]

26.2 Ahadith on dhikr and its numerous benefits

The Prophet (SAW) said:

"The comparison of the one who remembers Allah and the one who does not remember Allah is like that of the living and the dead."

[Bukhari, 11/208; Muslim, 1/539]

He (SAW) also said:

"Should I not inform you of the best of deeds, and the most sanctifying of deeds before your Lord, which does more to raise your positions (with Him), and is better for you than the disbursement of gold and money, or battle with the enemy?" They (the companions) said: "Indeed inform us." He (SAW) then said: "Remembrance of Allah."

[Narrated by At-Tirmidhi, 5/459; Ibn Maajah, 2/1245]

The Prophet (SAW) also said: Allah says:

"Indeed I am as My servant presumes Me to be, and I am with him when he remembers Me. So if he remembers Me to himself I remember him to Myself, and if he remembers Me amongst a company, I remember him amongst a company greater than it. And if he draws near to Me a span of a hand, I draw near to him the span of an arm, and if he draws near to me the span of an arm, I draw near to him the span of two outstretched arms, and if he takes a step towards Me I hastily step towards him."

[Narrated by Al-Bukhari 5/175; Muslim, 4/2061]

On the authority of Abdullah Ibn Busr (RA):

A man said to the Prophet (SAW): "O Messenger of Allah, the rights of Islam are much for me, so tell me of something that I might hold fast to." He (SAW) said: "Let not your tongue cease from the remembrance of Allah."
[Narrated by At-Tirmidhi, 5/458; Ibn Maajah, 2/1246]

The Prophet (SAW) also said:

"Whoever recites a letter of Allah's Book has for it, a merit and ten more like it, not to say that Alif, laam, meem are one letter but rather Alif is a letter, laam is a letter and meem is a letter."
[Narrated by At-Tirmidhi, 5/175]

He (SAW) also said:

"Are there any of you who would wish to go every day to *Buthaan* or *Al-'Aqeeq* (i.e. the name of two ditches in Madina), in the early morning and return from it with two she-camels without incurring any sin or severing relations?" We the companions said: "We would indeed love that, O Messenger of Allah." He (SAW) said: "Then you should go to the mosque and acquire some knowledge, or recite two verses from the Book of Allah, that would be better for you than two she-camels, and four verses are better than four she-camels and the same for a like number of male camels."
[Narrated by Muslim, 1/553]

The Prophet (SAW) also said:

"Whoever takes a seat and fails to remember Allah, has incurred upon himself a loss from Allah, and whoever

lies down (relaxes) and fails to remember Allah, has incurred upon himself a loss from Allah."

[Narrated by Abu Dawood, 4/264]

He (SAW) also said:

"Whenever a people sit in a gathering in which they fail to remember Allah and send prayers upon the Prophet (SAW) they incur a loss upon themselves and if Allah willed He would punish them and if He willed He would forgive them."

[Narrated by At-Tirmidhi, 3/140]

Similarly, he (SAW) said:

"Whenever a people rise from a gathering in which they failed to remember Allah, they rise as if they have arisen from the corpse of an ass and incurring upon themselves grief."

[Narrated by Abu Dawood, 4/264; Ahmad, 2/389; Saheeh Al-Jaami, 5/176]

Abu Huraira (RA) narrated that Allah's Apostle said:

"Shall I not tell you a thing, which, by doing, you will catch up with those who are ahead of you and supersede those who will come after you; and nobody will be able to do such a good deed as you do except the one who does the same? (deed as you do). That deed is to recite 'Subhanallah (Glory be to Allah) ten times, Alhamdulillah (Praise be to Allah) ten times and Allaho Akbar (Allah is the Greatest) ten times after every prayer.'"

[Narrated by Saheeh Al-Bukhari Volume VIII, The Book of Invocation, 6329]

Abu Musa (RA) narrated that Allah's Apostle said:

"O Abdullah bin Qais! Shall I teach you a sentence which is from the treasures of Paradise? It is "La haula wala quwwata illa bil-lah" (there is neither might nor power except with Allah)."
[Narrated by Saheeh Al-Bukhari Volume VIII, The Book of Invocation 6384]

Abu Huraira (RA) narrated that Allah's Apostle said:

"There are two expressions which are very easy for the tongue to say, but they are very heavy in the balance and are very dear to The Benficent (Allah), and they are 'Subhan Allah Al- Azim' and 'Subhan Allah wa bihamdihi' (I deem Allah free of any resemblance to anything what-so-ever in any respect and I celebrate His Praises.)"

26.3 Views of Scholars on dhikr

Ibn Al-Qayyim (RH) said in Madaarij Al-Saalikeen [2/244-246]:

Gratitude is based on five foundations: humility of the thankful one towards the One Who is thanked, his love for Him, his acknowledgement of His blessing, his praise of Him for that and not using it for anything that He hates.

It is narrated that the Prophet (SAW) taught people various adhkaar to say, and the best of dhikr is Laa ilaaha ill-Allah.

This is what he urged his paternal uncle Abu Taalib to say when he was dying. He said,

"O uncle, say Laa ilaaha ill-Allah and I will defend you thereby before Allah."

And he said,

"I know of a word which no one says when he is dying but his soul finds rest in it."

And he said,

"Anyone whose last words are Laa ilaaha ill-Allah will enter Paradise."

And he said,

"Whoever dies knowing that there is no god except Allah will enter Paradise."

And there are many similar ahadith.

[Majmoo' Al-Fataawaa, 10/556-558]

27 Virtues of Quran and impact on our Dua and relationship with Allah

One may wonder about the connection between Quran and dua. Quran is merely the words of Allah and He has termed it as a healing-tool for mankind. Quran, thus, can be used for physical as well as spiritual remedies.

Ibn al-Qayyim (may Allah have mercy on him) said:

> *We and others have tried this on many occasions and we have seen that it works in ways that physical remedies do not. Indeed we now regard physical medicine as the doctors regard folk medicine. This is in accordance with the law of divine wisdom, not contrary to it, but the causes of healing are many and varied. When the heart is in contact with the Lord of the Worlds, the Creator of the disease and the remedy, the Controller of nature Who directs it as He wills, he has other remedies apart from the remedies that are sought by the heart that is far away from Him and that turns away from Him. It is known that when a person's spirits are high and his body is in good shape, they cooperate in warding off disease and suppressing it, so if a person is in high spirits and physical good shape, finds comfort in being close to his Creator, loving Him, enjoying remembrance of Him (dhikr), devoting all his strength and power for His sake and focusing on Him, seeking His help, putting his trust in Him, how can anyone deny that this is the greatest medicine or that this spiritual power gives him the means to ward off pain and defeat it completely? No one would deny this but the most ignorant of people, those who are furthest away from Allah and the most hard-hearted and unaware of human nature.*

The remainder of this section highlights some virtues of Quran as they are mentioned in the Quran and Ahadith of the Prophet (SAW).

27.1 Quran on "Virtues of the Quran"

1. Alif-Lam-Meem. (These letters are one of the miracles of the Quran and none but Allah (alone) knows their meanings).

2. This is the Book (the Quran), whereof there is no doubt, a guidance to those who are Al-Muttaqoon (the pious and righteous persons who fear Allah much (abstain from all kinds of sins and evil deeds which He has forbidden) and love Allah much (perform all kinds of good deeds which He has ordained)).

3. Who believe in the Ghaib and perform As-Salat (Iqamat-as-Salat), and spend out of what we have provided for them (i.e. give Zakat , spend on themselves, their parents, their children, their wives, etc., and also give charity to the poor and Also in Allahs Cause, etc.).

4. And who believe in (the Quran and the Sunnah) which has been sent down (revealed) to you (Muhammad (SAW)) and in (the Taurat (Torah) and the Injeel (Gospel), etc.) which were sent down before you and they believe with certainty in the Hereafter (Resurrection, recompense of their good and bad deeds, Paradise and Hell, etc.).

5. They are on (true) guidance from their Lord, and they are the successful.

[Surah Al-Baqarah, 2:1- 5]

27.2 The word of the Lord of the worlds

Quran is the word of the Lord of the worlds, Allah, who revealed it to His messenger Muhammad, to guide and to bring mankind out of the darkness into the light:

> *"It is He, Who sends down manifest ayat (proofs, evidences, verses, lessons, signs, revelations, etc.) to His slave (Muhammad (SAW)) that He may bring you out from darkness into light. And verily, Allah is to you full of kindness, Most Merciful."*
>
> [Surah Al-Hadid, 57:9]

> *"And (remember) the Day when We shall raise up from every nation, a witness against them from amongst themselves. And We shall bring you (O Muhammad (SAW)) as a witness against these. And We have sent down to you the Book (the Quran), as an exposition of everything, a guidance, a mercy, and glad tidings for those who have submitted themselves (to Allah as Muslims)."*
>
> [Surah An-Nahl, 16:89]

27.3 Quran as a divine healing-tool and a source of mercy

Allah describes the Quran as 'a healing-tool and a source of mercy for the believers'.

It begins with Surah 'Fatiha', with praise of Allah, Lord of the worlds, followed by the believer's supplications to the Creator of all mankind to guide us on the Straight Path. The rest of the Quran provides guidance, which makes it possible for man to lead his life in the manner acceptable to his Creator and Sustainer.

"Perform As-Salat (Iqamat-as-Salat) from mid-day till the darkness of the night (i.e. the Zuhr, Asr, Maghrib, and Isha prayers), and recite the Quran in the early dawn (i.e. the morning prayer). Verily, the recitation of the Quran in the early dawn is ever witnessed (attended by the angels in charge of mankind of the day and the night).

[Surah Al-Isra, 17:78]

And We send down from the Quran that which is a healing and a mercy to those who believe (in Islamic Monotheism and act on it), and it increases the Zalimoon (polytheists and wrong-doers) nothing but loss.

[Surah Al-Isra, 17:82]

Say: "If the mankind and the jinns were together to produce the like of this Quran, they could not produce the like thereof, even if they helped one another."

[Surah Al-Isra, 17:88]

And indeed We have fully explained to mankind, in this Quran, every kind of similitude, but most mankind refuse (the truth and accept nothing) but disbelief.

[Surah Al-Isra, 17:89]

27.4 The rewards of reciting Quran in Qiyaam Al-Layl (Night prayers before Fajr)

We all know from the Quran and the Ahadeeth about the countless rewards and benefits of praying and reciting Quran during the nightly prayers (last one-third part of the night).

As is stated in the hadeeth narrated by 'Abd-Allah ibn 'Amr ibn al-'Aas (may Allah be pleased with them both), in which the Prophet (peace and blessings of Allah be upon him) said:

Whoever recites ten aayaat (verses) in qiyaam will not be recorded as one of the forgetful. Whoever recites a hundred aayaat (verses) in qiyaam will be recorded as one of the devout, and whoever prays a thousand aayaat (verses) in qiyaam will be recorded as one of the muqantareen (those who pile up good deeds)." (Reported by Abu Dawood and Ibn Hibbaan. It is a hasan report. Saheeh al-Targheeb, 635).

27.5 Reciting Quran in Ramadan

Quran has even more of an important significance in the month of Ramadan, the month of fasting. Allah says (interpretation of the meaning):

The month of Ramadan in which was revealed the Quran, a guidance for mankind and clear proofs for the guidance and the criterion (between right and wrong) [Quran aI-Baqarah 2:185]

Jibreel used to come to the Prophet (peace and blessings of Allah be upon him) every night in Ramadaan, and study the Quran with him. Narrated by al-Bukhaari, 5; Muslim, 4268.

27.6 Benefits of reciting certain Quranic surahs (chapters)

The following are authentic Ahadeeth regarding the benefits of certain Surahs. It was narrated from Abu Hurayrah that the Prophet (peace and blessings of Allah be upon him) said:

There is a soorah of the Quran containing thirty verses which have interceded for a man until he was forgiven. It is the soorah Tabaarak alladhi bi yadihi'l-mulk. Narrated by al-Tirmidhi, 2891; Ahmad, 7634; Abu Dawood, 1400; Ibn Maajah, 3786. This hadeeth was classed as hasan by al-Tirmidhi and by al-Albaani in Saheeh al-Tirmidhi, 3/6.

Regarding the healing power of Surah al-Fatiha, it was narrated that Abu Sa'eed (may Allah be pleased with him) said:

"A group of the companions of the Prophet (peace and blessings of Allah be upon him) set out on a journey and traveled until they stopped in (the land of) one of the Arab tribes. They asked them for hospitality but they refused to welcome them. The chief of that tribe was stung by a scorpion and they tried everything but nothing helped them. Some of them said, 'Why don't you go to those people who are camped (near us), maybe you will find something with them.' So they went to them and said, 'O people, our chief has been stung by a scorpion and we have tried everything but nothing helped him. Can any of you do anything?' One of them said, 'Yes, by Allah, I will recite ruqyah for him, but by Allah we asked you for hospitality and you did not welcome us, so I will not recite ruqyah for you until you give us something in return.' Then they agreed upon a flock of sheep.' Then he went and spat drily and recited over him Al-hamdu Lillaahi Rabb il-'Aalameen [Soorat al-Faatihah]. (The chief) got up as if he was released from a chain and started walking, and there were no signs of sickness on him. They paid them what they agreed to pay. Some of them (i.e. the companions) then suggested to divide their earnings among themselves, but the one who performed the ruqyah said, 'Do not divide them until we go to the Prophet (peace and blessings of Allah be upon him) and tell him what happened, then wait and see what he tells us to do.' So they went to the Messenger of Allah (peace and blessings of Allah be upon him) and told him what had happened. The Messenger of Allah (peace and blessings of Allah be

upon him) asked, 'How did you know that it (al-Faatihah) is a ruqyah?' Then he added, 'You have done the right thing. Share out (the flock of sheep) and give me a share too.' And the Messenger of Allah (peace and blessings of Allah be upon him) smiled." Narrated by al-Bukhaari, 2156; Muslim, 2201

A note about certain fabricated Ahadeeths narrating the benefits of some Quran Soorahs

Although there are authentic Ahadeeth regarding the rewards and benefits of reciting certain Quranic Surahs, unfortunately there are even more fabricated Ahadeeth that highlight the benefits of other Surahs. Therefore, not all Ahadeeth highlighting the benefits of reciting all Soorahs are authentic, even though some of those Ahadeeth mention a chain of narrators. Many scholars have proven the weakness of the narration chain of those Ahadeeth. As quoted at islam-qa.com, "Many ahaadeeth were fabricated about the virtues of various soorahs of the Quran. Their fabricators' intention was to encourage people to read Quran and to devote themselves to that, and they claimed that they were doing good thereby. But their intentions were misguided because that is undoubtedly subject to the stern warning contained in the words of the Prophet (peace and blessings of Allah be upon him): "Whoever tells a lie about me deliberately, let him take his place in Hell." Narrated by al-Bukhaari, 10; Muslim, 4. It makes no difference whether the lie is intended for good or for evil."

27.7 A Muslim's status is raised by the Quran

A Musilm's status is raised by the Quran. So, the more you recite Quran and follow its commandments and make Quran an integral part of your life, the more Allah will elevate your status in this life and the hereafter.

Saheeh Muslim mentions a story where some men came to question Umar ibn Al-Khattaab during his khilaafah about the leadership of Makkah, they asked, "Who do you use to govern Makkah?" He said, "Ibn Abzaa." They asked, "And who is Ibn Abzaa?" Umar replied, "A freed slave from those we freed." They remarked, "You left a freed slave in charge of the people of the Valley (the noble tribes of the Quraysh)!?!?" So he answered them, "Verily he is a reader of the Book of Allah and is knowledgeable about the obligations of the Muslims. Haven't you heard the statement of your Messenger: "Verily Allah raises some people by this Book and lowers others by it."

'Uthmaan, may Allah be pleased with him, said that the Prophet (sallAllahu 'alaihi wa sallam) said:

The best of you are the ones who learn the Qur'an and teach it to others" [Al-Bukhari]

Narrated Aisha: The Prophet said,

Such a person who recites the Quran and masters it by heart, will be with the noble righteous scribes (in Heaven). And such a person exerts himself to learn the Quran by heart, and recites it with great difficulty, will have a double reward." (book #60, Hadith #459)

27.8 Allah's gift of guidance

The Quran is the Book of Allah for all of mankind:

"Verily, We have sent down to you (O Muhammad (SAW)) the Book (this Quran) for mankind in truth. So whosoever accepts the guidance, it is only for his own self, and whosoever goes astray, he goes astray only for

his (own) loss. And you (O Muhammad (SAW)) are not a
Wakeel (trustee or disposer of affairs, or keeper) over
them."

[Surah Al-Zumar, 39:41]

27.9 Allah's final revelation to mankind

Muslims believe that Quran is in its exact form as it was revealed by
Allah on Prophet Muhammad (SAW). All other revealed books
except the Quran have been changed and distorted over the time.
The Quran is and will remain, intact in its original form till the Day of
Judgment. Allah has sent down Quran to us and has guaranteed to
preserve it, taking upon Himself the responsibility of preserving it till
the last day. Allah says:

"It is We Who have sent down the Dhikr (i.e. the Quran)
and surely, We will guard it (from corruption)."

[Surah Al-Hijr, 13:19]

The Quran is the only religious sacred writing that has been in
circulation for such a long time and yet remains as pure as it was
revealed. It has been kept intact. Nothing has been added to it;
nothing has been changed in it; and nothing has been taken away
from it, ever since its revelation more than 1400 years ago.

"And this Quran is not such as could ever be produced
by other than Allah (Lord of the heavens and the earth),
but it is a confirmation of (the revelation) which was
before it (i.e. the Taurat (Torah), and the Injeel (Gospel),
etc.), and a full explanation of the Book (i.e. laws and
orders, etc, decreed for mankind) - wherein there is no
doubt from the Lord of the alameen (mankind, jinns,and
all that exists)."

[Surah Yunus, 10:37]

The Quran calls upon humanity to examine and to ponder over the signs of Allah in the universe and in the Verses of the Quran:

"Say: "Behold all that is in the heavens and the earth," but neither ayat (proofs, evidences, verses, lessons, signs, revelations, etc.) nor warners benefit those who believe not."

[Surah Yunus, 10:101]

"Do they not then think deeply in the Quran, or are their hearts locked up (from understanding it)?"

[Surah Muhammad, 47:24]

Allah says:

"Had We sent down this Quran on a mountain, you would surely have seen it humbling itself and rending asunder by the fear of Allah. Such are the parables, which We put forward to mankind that they may reflect."

[Surah Al-Hashr, 58:21]

27.10 The greatest miracle of Prophet Muhammad (SAW)

Allah has declared that there is nothing like the Quran and He has challenged others to produce anything similar to it. Allah says in the Quran:

"And if you (Arab Pagans, Jews, and Christians) are in doubt concerning that, which We have sent down (i.e. the Quran) to Our slave (Muhammad (SAW)), then produce a Surah (chapter) of the like thereof and call your witnesses (supporters and helpers) besides Allah, if you are truthful."

[Surah Al-Baqarah, 2:23]

Allah has challenged the mankind and the jinn to produce something like it, even one surah or one aayah (verse), but they could not and will never be able to do that, as Allah says:

Say: "If the mankind and the jinns were together to produce the like of this Quran, they could not produce the like thereof, even if they helped one another."

[Surah Al-Isra, 17:88]

27.11   Ahadith on the "Virtues of Quran"

The following are some of the ahadith highlighting the virtues of the Quran.

Abu Huraira (RA) narrated: The Prophet (SAW) said:

"Every Prophet (SAW) was given miracles because of which people believed, but what I have been given is Divine Inspiration which Allah has revealed to me. So I hope that my followers will out-number the followers of the other Prophets (AS) on the Day of Resurrection."
[Narrated by Saheeh Al-Bukhari: The Book of the Virtues of the Quran, 4981]

Abu Sa'id Al-Mu'Alla narrated: The Prophet (SAW) said:

"Shall I not teach you the most superior Surah in the Quran?" He said: (It is) "Praise be to Allah, the Lord of the worlds" i.e. Surah Fatiha which consists of seven repeatedly recited Verses and the Magnificent Quran was given to me."
[Narrated by Saheeh Al-Bukhari: The Book of the Virtues of the Quran, 5006]

Abu Mas'ud narrated: The Prophet (SAW) said:

"If somebody recites the last two Verses of Surah Al-Baqara at night, that will be sufficient for him."
[Narrated by Saheeh Al-Bukhari: The Book of the Virtues of the Quran, 5009]

Umar bin Al-Khattab narrated that the Prophet (SAW) said:

"Tonight there has been revealed to me a Surah which is dearer to me than that on which the sun shines (i.e. the world)." Then he (SAW) recited: "Verily! We have given you (O Muhammad (SAW)) manifest victory." [Surah Al-Fath, 48:1]
[Narrated by Saheeh Al-Bukhari: The Book of the Virtues of the Quran, 5012]

Abu Sa'id Al-Khudri (RA) narrated:

A man heard another man reciting: "Say. He is Allah, (the) One." [Surah Al-Ikhlas, 112:1] repeatedly. The next morning he came to Allah's Apostle (SAW) and informed him about it as if he thought that it was not enough to recite. On that Allah's Apostle (SAW) said: "By Him in Whose Hand my life is, this Surah is equal to one-third of the Quran!"
[Narrated by Saheeh Al-Bukhari: The Book of the Virtues of the Quran, 5013]

Aisha (RA) narrated:

Whenever Allah's Apostle (SAW) became sick, he would recite Surah Al-Falaq and Surah An-Nas and then blow his breath over his body. When he became seriously ill, I used to recite (these two Surahs) and rub his hands over his body for its blessings.

[Narrarted by Saheeh Al-Bukhari: The Book of the Virtues of the Quran, 5016]

Aisha (RA) narrated:

> *Whenever Allah's Apostle (SAW) went to bed every night, he used to cup his hands together and blow over it after reciting Surah Al-Ikhlas, Surah Al-Falaq and Surah An-Nas, and then rub his hands over whatever parts of his body he was able to rub, starting with his head, face, and front of his body. He used to do that three times.*
> [Narrated by Saheeh Al-Bukhari: The Book of the Virtues of the Quran, 5017]

Uthman bin Affan (RA) narrated: The Prophet (SAW) said:

> *"The most superior among you (Muslims) are those who learn the Quran and teach it."*
> [Narrated by Saheeh Al-Bukhari: The Book of the Virtues of the Quran, 5028]

It was narrated from Abu Hurayrah that the Prophet (SAW) said:

> *"A surah from the Quran containing thirty verses will intercede for a man so that he will be forgiven. It is the Surah Tabaarak Alathi bi yadihi'l-mulk [i.e., Surah Al-Mulk]."*
> [Narrated by Al-Tirmidhi, 2891; Abu Dawood, 1400; Ibn Maajah, 3786. Al-Tirmidhi said, this is a hasan hadith. It was classed as Saheeh by Shaykh Al-Islam Ibn Taymiyah in Majmoo' Al-Fataawa, 22/277 and by Shaykh Al-Albaani in Saheeh Ibn Maajah, 3053]

What is evident from these ahadith is that a person should read it every night, and act in accordance with the rulings contained in it, and believe in the information mentioned in it.

It was narrated that 'Abd-Allah ibn Mas'ood said:

> *Whoever reads Tabaarak Allahi bi yadihi'l-mulk [i.e., Surah Al-Mulk] every night, Allah will protect him from the torment of the grave. At the time of the Messenger of Allah, we used to call it Al-maani'ah (that which protects). In the Book of Allah it is a surah which, whoever recites it every night has done very well.*
> [Narrated by Al-Nasaa'i, 6/179; classed as hasan by Al-Albaani in Saheeh Al-Targheeb wa'l-Tarheeb, 1475]

Gatherings in which the Quran is recited and studied, whereby one person recites the Holy Quran, while the the others listen and then they study it together and explain the meanings, is something that is prescribed in Islam and is an act of worship that Allah loves and for which He rewards greatly.

It was narrated by Muslim in his Saheeh and by Abu Dawood from Abu Hurayrah (RA) that the Prophet (SAW) said:

> *"No people gather in one of the houses of Allah, reciting the Book of Allah and studying it together, but tranquility descends upon them and mercy encompasses them, and the angels surround them, and Allah mentions them to those who are with Him."*

28 Dua stories of the Prophets mentioned in the Quran

This section recounts some of the stories of the prophets that are mentioned in the Quran and how they made dua on different occasions for their needs. Although each story is mentioned briefly, the section is meant to demonstrate by examples of how the lives of the prophets revolved around maintaining their relationship with Allah by constantly asking Him for their needs and seeking His guidance in their affairs. This should help us to inculcate the same discipline and habits of dua, as is explained in these short accounts.

28.1 Prophet Adam's Dua on showing his remorse for wrongdoing

Allah (SWT) accepted dua of the prophets. The first man and Prophet of Allah was Prophet Adam, who lived in paradise with his wife Hawwa. Allah (SWT) asked the angels to bow down to Prophet Adam but Satan refused out of pride and haughtiness. He not only disobeyed Allah but also instigated Prophet Adam into disobeying Allah and eating the fruit of the tree which Allah had forbidden. Though Prophet Adam was misled into disobeying Allah, he was filled with remorse at his action and repented sincerely. Allah showed His Mercy and revealed the words seeking forgiveness from Him. Prophet Adam repeated these words and he was forgiven. The Dua of Prophet Adam was:

> *"Our Lord! We have wronged ourselves. If You forgive us not, and bestow not upon us Your Mercy, we shall certainly be of the losers. (Quran: Chapter of Al-A'raf; 7:23)*

28.2 Prophet Nuh on being accused of falsehood

Prophet Nuh was another Prophet of Allah who was instructed by Allah (SWT) to propagate the message of Allah's Oneness. But when he told his people to worship Allah alone and lead righteous lives, they refused to listen to him or accept him as a Prophet, attributing altogether wrong motives to him. They accused him of trying to establish his own personal superiority over them by his preaching. They also accused him of falsehood in claiming to bring a message from Allah. They argued that if Allah had wished to send them messengers, He would have sent angels, not a man like themselves and from among themselves. They were adamant on not worshipping One God, as their ancestors had not done so. Some accused Prophet Nuh of madness and said he should be left alone for his madness to run out. In anguish, Prophet Nuh prayed to Allah for help:

"O my Lord! Help me; for that they accuse me of falsehood!" (Quran: Chapter of Al-Mu'minun; 23:26)

Allah answered his prayers and instructed Prophet Nuh to construct an Ark under His Guidance. He also instructed him to take on board with him pairs of all species, male and female, and his own family except his wife and son who were among those who doubted him.

Prophet Nuh followed Allah's injunctions and Allah (SWT) saved him and the believers with him from the deluge which drowned the disbelievers and tormentors of Prophet Nuh. For a safe landing, Prophet Nuh was instructed by Allah to praise Him and offer this supplication:

"And say: 'My Lord! Cause me to land at a blessed landing- place, for You are the Best of those who bring to land.'"(Quran: Chapter of Al-Mu'minun; 23:29)

28.3 Prophet Ibrahim's Dua for the protection of his family and the Muslim Ummah

Prophet Ibrahim was convinced about the Oneness of Allah and denounced idolatry. He was chosen by Allah to sanctify the Ka'abah.

Once, Prophet Ibrahim had to leave his wife and infant son Ismail in a valley near the Ka'abah under a tree on the spot of *zamzam*. During those days Makkah was not populated nor was there any water. So he made them sit there and placed near them a leather bag containing some dates, and a small water skin containing some water and set out homeward. He sought Allah's protection for his wife and son with this supplication:

> *"O our Lord! I have made some of my offspring to dwell in an uncultivable valley by Your Sacred House in order that they may perform As-Salat. So fill some hearts among men with love towards them, and (O Allah) provide them with fruits so that they may give thanks."(Ibrahim; 14:37)*

Allah answered his prayer and made water spring from the spot where the little child Ismail was rubbing his feet. Later some people passed by, saw the water and settled in the valley with their families.

Later in life, while he and his son Prophet Ismail were raising the foundations of Ka'bah, Prophet Ibrahim prayed the following to to Allah:

..........."Our Lord! Accept (this service) from us. Verily! You are the All-Hearer, the All-Knower."

"Our Lord! And make us submissive unto You and of our offspring a nation submissive unto You, and show us our Manasik (all the ceremonies of pilgrimage - Hajj and Umrah, etc.), and accept our repentance. Truly, You are the One Who accepts repentance, the Most Merciful.

"Our Lord! Send amongst them a Messenger of their own (and indeed Allah answered their invocation by sending Muhammad Peace be upon him), who shall recite unto them Your Verses and instruct them in the Book (this Quran) and Al-Hikmah (full knowledge of the Islamic laws and jurisprudence or wisdom or Prophethood, etc.), and sanctify them. Verily! You are the All-Mighty, the All-Wise." (Chapter of Al-Baqarah; 2:127-129)

Allah (SWT) answered Prophet Ibrahim's supplication by sending the Messenger Muhammad (SAWS) and revealing to him the Quran which contains full knowledge of the Islamic laws, jurisprudence and wisdom.

"And We bestowed on him (Ibrahim (Abraham)), Ishaque (Isaac) and Yaqoob (Jacob), and ordained among his offspring Prophethood and the Book (i.e. the Taurat (Torah) (to Moosa Moses), the Injeel (Gospel) (to Iesa Jesus), the Quran (to Muhammad SAW), all from the offspring of Ibrahim (Abraham)), and We granted him his reward in this world, and verily, in the Hereafter he is indeed among the righteous." (Al-Ankabut; 29:27)

28.4 Prophet Lut's Dua for people who had belied him

Prophet Lut was a nephew of Prophet Ibrahim and was sent as a Prophet and warning to the people of Sodom and Gomorrah. These cities were utterly destroyed for their unspeakable sins. He adhered to Prophet Ibrahim's teaching and faith and accepted voluntary exile with him, for Prophet Ibrahim left the home of his fathers. Prophet Lut tried to stop people from their lust of shameful crimes, which were against the laws of nature. These horrible crimes were committed openly and publicly, even in their assemblies. The people were so defiant and bent on polluting the earth with their crimes, that they paid no heed to Prophet Lut. Disbelieving in Allah and His Punishment, they dared Allah's prophet Lut (AS) to bring about the punishment if he could. He prayed to Allah:

> *"He said: "My Lord! Give me victory over the people who are Mufsidoon (those who commit great crimes and sins, oppressors, tyrants, mischief-makers, corrupts)."(Chapter of Al-Ankabut; 29:30)*

His prayer was answered and he was saved when his town with its entire population who belied him was destroyed by a 'Single mighty blast'. It was a terrible earthquake that buried the people and destroyed their boasted civilization.

28.5 Prophet Yakoob's Dua in the face of calamity

Prophet Yusuf was the son of Prophet Yakoob who was the grandson of Prophet Ibrahim. He was his father's favorite and his half-brothers were jealous of him. When he was young prophet Yusuf's brothers took him along with them, against their father's wishes and ultimately threw him in a well. They told their father that a wolf had eaten Yusuf. Prophet Yakoob was extremely patient and had total trust in Allah. On hearing the news he just said:

"……..And it is Allah (Alone) Whose help can be sought against that which you assert. (Chapter of Yusuf; 12:18)

Allah (SWT) rewarded him for his trust and Faith in Him, by uniting him with his lost son.

28.6 Prophet Yusuf's Dua on staying away from sins and to stay as a righteous person

When Prophet Yusuf was being accused of seducing the wife of the Aziz who had purchased him and treated him more like a guest and son than a slave, Prophet Yusuf invoked Allah, preferring to be imprisoned rather than staying among those who were plotting against him and suspecting his integrity and character:

"He said:"O my Lord! Prison is more to my liking than that to which they invite me. Unless You turn away their plot from me, I will feel inclined towards them and be one (of those who commit sin and deserve blame or those who do deeds) of the ignorants."

"So his Lord answered his invocation and turned away from him their plot. Verily, He is the All-Hearer, the All-Knower." (Chapter of Yusuf;12:33,34)

When Allah granted Prophet Yusuf dignity and supreme power under the king and brought his parents to him, he prayed:

"My Lord! You have indeed bestowed on me of the sovereignty, and taught me something of the interpretation of dreams – the (Only) Creator of the heavens and the earth! You are My Wali (Protector, Helper, Supporter, Guardian, God, Lord) in this world

and in the Hereafter. Cause me to die as a Muslim (the one submitting to Your Will), and join me with the righteous."(Chapter of Yusuf;12:101)

28.7 Prophet Shuayb's Dua on asking for Judgment

Prophet Shuayb was amongst the fourth generation of Prophet Ibrahim. His mission was in one of the settled towns of the Midianites. The Midianites were in the path of a commercial highway of Asia, between two opulent and highly organized nations as Egypt and the Mesopotamian group, comprising Assyria and Babylonia. Their besetting sins were giving short measure or weight, depriving people of rightful dues, producing mischief and disorder and giving in to highway robbery. Prophet Shuayb came as a peace maker to Madyan, which was torn by internal conflict. He appealed to the people to worship Allah, to give just measure and weight, to give people their rightful dues and to stay away from mischief. But the arrogant people threatened to drive him out if he did not return to their ways and religion. He prayed to Allah to decide between him and them and Allah answered his prayer:

"We should have invented a lie against Allah if we returned to your religion, after Allah has rescued us from it. And it is not for us to return to it unless Allah, our Lord, should will. Our Lord comprehends all things in His Knowledge. In Allah (Alone) we put our trust. Our Lord! Judge between us and our people in truth, for You are the Best of those who give judgment." (Chapter of Al-A'raf;7: 89)

So the earthquake seized them and they lay (dead), prostrate in their homes."(Chapter of Al-A'raf;7:91)

28.8 Prophet's Musa's Dua in making his tasks easy against Pharaoh

The year when Prophet Musa was born, the Pharoah had ordered that every new-born son of the tribe of Israel should be killed, as it had been prophesied by his sooth-sayers that a child would be born in an Israeli family who would be the cause of his destruction and bring an end to his reign. As a consequence of this decree, Musa (AS) was hidden for three months after he was born. When he could be hidden no longer, he was put into an ark of bulrushes and cast into the Nile, where he was found by the Pharaoh's wife and daughter and adopted into the family. When he grew up he was chosen by Allah to deliver his people from the Pharoah's cruelties. Allah ordered him to point out the error of the Pharoah's ways to him. The Pharoah would tell his subjects that he was their Lord Most High.

Prophet Musa prayed to Allah:

"O my Lord! Open for me my chest (grant me self-confidence ,contentment and boldness)

"And ease my task for me;
"And loose the knot (the defect) from my tongue, (i.e. remove the incorrectness from my speech)

"That they understand my speech.
"And appoint for me a helper from my family,
"Harun (Aaron), my brother.
"Increase my strength with him,
"And let him share my task (of conveying Allah's Message and Prophethood),

"That we may glorify You much,
"And remember You much,
"Verily You are a Well-Seer of us."

(Chapter of Ta-"Ha; 20:25-35)

Allah accepted Prophet Musa's supplication:

> *"(Allah) said: You are granted your request, O Musa!"*
> *(Chapter of Ta-"Ha; 20:36)*

28.9 Prophet Ayub's Dua in the face of severe distress

Prophet Ayub was a prosperous man with faith in Allah. He suffered from a number of tests from Allah. His cattle were destroyed and his family crushed under his roof. As a further test, he was covered with loathsome sores from head to foot. But he held fast to his faith in Allah. He was a brilliant example of patience through which he became a great Prophet of Allah, and he was ever-trustful of Him and His promises. With his humility, patience and faith in Allah he fought and conquered evil. When he invoked Allah in his distress, Allah answered his prayers and removed the distress.

> *"And Ayub, when he cried to his Lord: Verily distress has seized me, and You are the Most Merciful of all those who show mercy."*

> *"So We answered his call, and We removed the distress that was on him, and We restored his family to him (that he had lost) and the like thereof along with them as a mercy from Ourselves and a Reminder for all those who worship Us." (Chapter of Al-Anbiya; 21:83, 84)*

28.9.1 Prophet Yunus's Dua in accepting his weakness during calamities

Prophet Yunus was the Prophet raised to warn the Assyrian capital Nineveh, steeped in wickedness. He was rejected by the people. When they did not pay heed to his first warning he denounced

Allah's wrath on them. But they repented and Allah forgave them for the time being. Meanwhile Prophet Yunus departed in wrath, discouraged at the apparent failure of his mission, forgetting that Allah has Mercy as well as forgiveness. Prophet Yunus went away to the sea and took a ship. The ship was fully laden and met foul weather. The sailors according to their superstition wanted to find out who was responsible for the ill-luck. The lot fell on Prophet Yunus and he was cast off. He was swallowed by a big fish but in the depth of darkness, he cried to Allah and confessed his weakness. Allah Most Gracious accepted his supplication and forgave him. He was cast ashore, given the shelter of a plant and was refreshed and strengthened. He continued his mission and his work prospered. Thus he overcame all his disappointments by repentance and Faith and Allah accepted him.

> *"And (remember)Yunus , when he went off in anger, and imagined that We shall not punish him (i.e. the calamities which had befallen him)! But he cried through the darkness (saying): 'None has the right to be worshipped but You (O Allah), Glorified (and Exalted) are You! Truly, I have been of the wrong-doers."*

> *"So We answered his call, and delivered him from the distress. And thus We do deliver the believers."*
> *(Chapter of Al-Anbiya; 21:87, 88)*

28.9.2 Prophet Zakariyyah's Dua in seeking righteous children

Prophet Zakariya was a priest of Allah. Both he and his wife were devout in their duties towards Allah. They were old and did not have a son. His relatives were his colleagues. But he found in them no true spirit of service for Allah and his men. He feared that his own family and relatives were going wrong and he wanted to keep the lamp of Allah's message burning bright. He was filled with anxiety as to who would uphold the goodly ideas he had in mind, which seemed strange to his worldly colleagues. He expressed his anguish at not having any child and prayed to Allah for a son – not out of selfishness, but for a public need, in the service of Allah. He was too old, but wanted to have an heir to whom he could transmit his most precious possessions - his character and virtue, as a man of Allah. Allah (SWT) answered his prayers and gave him a son, Prophet Yahya, who added to the devout reputation of the family for he is called "noble, chaste, and a Prophet". All three, father, mother and son, were made worthy of each other, and they repelled evil by their virtue and piety.

> *"And (remember) Zakariyya, when he cried to his Lord: 'O My Lord! Leave me not alone, Thou are the Best of inheritors."*

> *"And We answered his call, and We bestowed on him Yahya, and cured his wife (to bear a child) for him. Verily, they used to hasten on to do good deeds, and they used to call on Us with hope and fear, and used to humble themselves before Us." (Chapter of Al-Anbiya; 21:89,90)*

28.9.3 Prophet Dawood's Dua in the face of trials

Prophet Dawood was a king and a Prophet of Allah. Allah had given him wisdom and sound judgment. One day, two men came to seek justice from him. They were brothers who wanted him to settle their quarrel. One of them complained that he had one ewe and his brother who had ninety-nine ewes wanted him to give him the one that he had. Prophet Dawood (AS) spoke to them about falsehood and the fraud of men who should be content with what they had, but who covet more. Especially, he said, it is wrong for brothers or men in partnership to take advantage of each other; but how few are the men who are righteous. At this moment Prophet Dawood (AS), realized that he was being tested for his moral and spiritual fiber.

Great though he was as a king, and just though he was as a judge, the moment that he thought of these things in self-pride, his merit vanished. In himself he was as other men; it was Allah's Grace that gave him wisdom and justice, and he should have been humble in the sight of Allah. He immediately sought Allah's forgiveness and his repentance was accepted:

> *"(Dawood (David)) said (immediately without listening to the opponent): "He has wronged you in demanding your ewe in addition to his ewes. And, verily, many partners oppress one another, except those who believe and do righteous good deeds, and they are few." And Dawood (David) guessed that We have tried him and he sought Forgiveness of his Lord, and he fell down prostrate and turned (to Allah) in repentance.*
>
> *So We forgave him that, and verily, for him is a near access to Us, and a good place of (final) return (Paradise)."(Chapter of Saad; 38:24,25)*

28.9.4 Prophet Sulaiman's Dua for a great kingdom

Prophet Sulaiman (alaihs'salam) was the son of Prophet Dawood (alaihis'salam). Like his father, he was also most meticulous in not allowing the least motive of self to be mixed up with his spiritual virtues. He was fond of horses, he had great armies and wealth but he used them all in Allah's service. His battles were not fought for lust of blood but for the cause to establish righteousness. His prayer to Allah that was answered was:

> *He said: "My Lord! Forgive me, and bestow upon me a kingdom such as shall not belong to any other after me: Verily, You are the Bestower."*
>
> *So, We subjected to him the wind, it blew gently to his order whithersoever he willed, And also the Shayatin*

(devils) from the jinns (including) every kind of builder and diver, And also others bound in fetters.
(Saying of Allah to Sulaiman (Solomon)): "This is Our gift, so spend you or withhold, no account will be asked."
And verily, he enjoyed a near access to Us, and a good final return (Paradise)." (Chapter of Saad;38:35-40)

28.10   Prophet Muhammad's Dua on facing difficulties

Prophet Muhammad (sallallahu alaihi va salaam) conveyed the Message of Allah to the people of Makkah. Although many people accepted him as a Prophet and followed his teachings, there were still many disbelievers who either set up partners with Allah or refused to believe that the Quran was the Divine revelation of Allah to Prophet (SAW). One of the Prophet's prayer that was answered by Allah(SWT) is mentioned in the Quran:

"Say (O Muhammad SAW): " My Lord! If You would show me that with which they are threatened (torment),

"My Lord! Then (save me from Your Punishment), and put me not amongst the people who are the Zalimoon (polytheists and wrong-doing)."

And indeed We are Able to show you (O Muhammad SAW) that with which We have threatened them." (Chapter of Al-Muminun; 23:93-95)

Prophet Muhammad's (SAW) Hijrah from Makkah and the eventual overthrow of the Makkan oligarchy amply prove the acceptance of his supplication to Allah (SWT).

29 Dua Checklist

This checklist is derived from the divine guidance mentioned earlier in this book. Keep this handy and refer to it often, until you fully inculcate this discipline in your life.

Remember –

- ✓ Dua is an act of worship. Make it at all the times to seek Allah's attention.

- ✓ Dua can cause miracles to happen.

- ✓ Use Allah's 99 names to call upon Him. For example, use "Allah" or "Rahman"

- ✓ Avoid haram food, provision and sins

- ✓ Preferably face the Qiblah when making dua

- ✓ Do not ask Allah for anything that is sinful in your dua

- ✓ Say a lot of istighfar during the day (the simplest form is to say AstaghfurAllah)

- ✓ Make dua during the last one-third part of the night

- ✓ Make dua after the prescribed prayers

- ✓ Make dua between the Adhan (call for prayers) and the Iqamah

- ✓ Make Dua at the time of rain

- ✓ Make plenty of dua on Fridays

- ✓ Engage in lot of Dhikr-Allah (remembrance of Allah)

THE POWER OF DUA

✓ Send a lot of blessings on Prophet (peace and blessings of Allah be upon him)

✓ Make dua with the help of the prayer of Dhun-Noon (Prophet Yoonus)

✓ Be focused and ask Allah with full conviction

✓ Be persistent in your dua and repeat it often

✓ Make a lot of dua when you are fasting or travelling

✓ Do NOT pray against oneself, wealth and children

30 References

1. The Noble Quran

2. Hadith Sahih Bukhari

3. Hadith Muslim

4. www.IqraSense.com

5. www.IslamQA.info

6. Qisas Al-Anbiyya

OTHER BOOKS BY IQRASENSE.COM

1. Dua for Success – 100+ Dua (supplications) for success and happiness
2. Jesus – The Prophet Who Didn't Die
3. Summarized Stories of the Quran
4. Jerusalem is "Ours" – The Christian, Islamic, and Jewish struggle for the "Holy Lands"

ABOUT THE AUTHOR

IqraSense.com is a blog covering religion topics on Islam and other religious topics. To discuss and read this topic in more detail, you are encouraged to join the discussion and provide your comments by visiting the blog.

--- **The End** ---

Made in the USA
Lexington, KY
11 November 2016